Gayma Sutra

Axel Neustädter is a freelance writer living in Berlin. He has ed-
ited the gay erotica series *Loverboys*, to which he also contributed
two novels. The *Gayma Sutra* is a further exploration of the topic
introduced in the bestselling *69 Positions of Joyful Gay Sex*, for
which he also wrote the text.

Axel Neustädter

GAYMA SUTRA

The Complete Guide to Sex Positions

BRUNO GMÜNDER

GAYMA SUTRA

1st Edition 2014
Copyright © 2014 Bruno Gmünder Group GmbH
Original title: Gaymasutra. Mehr Spaß mit den besten Sex-Stellungen
Text: © Axel Neustädter
Translation: Nicola Heine
Photo credits: page 187

Bruno Gmünder Group GmbH
Kleiststraße 23-26, 10787 Berlin
info@brunogmuender.com

Printed in Germany

ISBN 978-3-86787-792-3

Mor about our books and authors:
www.brunogmuender.com

For Felix, who started it all

Please note:

One of the reasons sex is so exciting is that not only is it different every time, it's also something to be re-discovered again with every new partner. That means: every date, every orgy, and every night of passion is determined by the distinct characteristics that make up its history and the people participating. It's always guaranteed to be one of a kind—but this can sometimes be a hindrance as well. Physique, temperament, physical fitness ... these factors determine the limits of every physical exchange.

What I'm trying to say is, even while encouraging you to test your personal limits within the pages of this book, I'm still asking you to respect them. Your own limits and those of your partner. Not everyone will be able to manage every position, and if it starts to hurt you should definitely stop. That can be a good thing, too: the point you stop at can also be the point you start again.

So before you start putting all you've read into practice, you should always ask yourself the following question: are you prepared to handle your sexual encounters responsibly, even in the absence of safe sex caveats and warnings not to overdo it jumping out at you from every page?

If your answer to this question is "yes," then welcome to the Gayma Sutra. If your answer is "no," then I suggest you either tear this book up or throw it out the window. You will do a lot less damage that way than if you act irresponsibly towards yourself or your partner.

CONTENTS

Part 1

Part 2

_____Preface: The Author's Position

When I was asked to write the text to _69 Positions of Joyful Gay Sex_ two years ago, I was thrilled. Not only was I interested in the subject matter, I also saw this as an opportunity for writing about sex and how to do it in a more documentary fashion than in my novels and short stories. Besides, it all sounded so easy. A bit of "stick your ass out" here and a bit of "stick your leg up" there—that ought to flow from my keyboard easily enough. So I accepted.

A couple of days later I was seated at my desk, racking my brain: in front of me a heap of photos of two porn stars in a completely empty apartment, acrobatically going through all kinds of positions, some of which I was familiar with in real life, others that just looked terribly uncomfortable. My personal highlight is still the "wheelbarrow," where the bottom supports himself on the floor with his forearms and twines his legs around the hips of the stud standing behind him and nailing him at the same time. Not having been present at the photo shoot, and as a member of the "Photoshop generation," I am somewhat suspicious of the general message of media images. As a consequence, I couldn't help but ask myself: is what those guys are doing even possible?

All of a sudden, I was beset by doubts as to my suitability for the task in hand. And I broke out in a sweat as the thought that I would ideally have to try out all sixty-nine positions myself in order to describe them adequately began to take hold. To calm myself down, I had a beer. Then I had another one. Then I picked up the phone and called my boyfriend. It was the middle of the afternoon and he was at work. I can still remember putting on my most dulcet and unthreatening voice to tell him: "Do you think you could swing by my place right after work? There's something I need to talk to you about."

His reply was nice enough, but not particularly helpful: "Have you been drinking or something?"

It can come as a shock to realize that after being together for two years, your partner can see straight through you. On the other hand, it saved me from having to beat around the bush. I gave him a brief rundown of the *Joyful Gay Sex* assignment and my sudden doubts and emphasized how important it was for us to try out at least a few of the "positions" at hand ourselves. If this conversation had taken place in one of my novels, the guy on the other end of the line would have been licking his lips in anticipation, but this was real life. So what was his reaction?

"Can't you do that with someone else?"

His reaction had nothing whatsoever to do with any lackluster quality in our sex life. While we had decided to open up the relationship after seven months of voluntary monogamy, and in theory were allowed to go to bed with other people, in practice, opening up the relationship had actually made our sex life more intimate. In our case, intimacy equaled pleasure. And pleasure equaled spontaneity. Dutifully choerographed fuck sessions weren't really our thing. At least, not up till then ...

Because, of course, my boyfried didn't turn down my request. And, of course, neither of us could stop thinking about the promise of our evening together, until we had both reached a frenzy of anticipation. Surprisingly enough, we did indeed have loads of fun trying out some of the positions. And when I say fun, I mean laughing, playing, and sharing thrills. Oddly enough, the explicit agreement we had reached in that phone call and the clear instructions provided by the photos meant that there was no pressure. We weren't trying to be especially romantic or particularly hot, but precisely because we weren't trying, after a short time, that is exactly what happened. Or to put it differently, at first our bodies were stiff, but our dicks were not, half an hour later the situation had been reversed, so we were able to "work" quite effectively. We did actually try out most of the positions on our list that same evening. Not for very long, for the most part, but all the same ...

After a while, we started getting ambitious. I have to admit though, the wheelbarrow was simply beyond our capabilities. To this day, reading the text that was printed later on still makes me laugh. It says: "The 'wheelbarrow' is a hard nut to crack for even the most adventurous couple. Or should I add 'and a easy way to crack a joint.' The fact is, it's a myth, but it can be done. But only with a lot of practice ..." We hadn't practiced. And with your dick pointing straight up at the ceiling, intercrural sex will probably be the best you can manage. But it's kind of early to start quibbling. What I'm trying to say in this long preface is this: if, upon hearing the words "sex positions" you just shake your head disdainfully, muttering "that kind of thing just happens by itself," then it's time to think again. Firstly: because you'll be missing out on a lot. Secondly: because far too many gay men flaunt this whole "I know everything anyway" attitude and it's never, ever justified. Thirdly: because there are some things that don't just happen by themselves. You don't just happen upon positions like the "fuckquake" or "suspended congress"—you have to try them out.

And it's definitely worth it. Because it gives you the opportunity to rediscover your own body and that of your partner. From my own experience, I can only say that trying out new positions injected a new dose of vitality and adventurousness into our sex life. I'm not going to make a secret of the fact that our relationship didn't last, but our breakup had nothing to do with any lack of erotic harmony; it was more about our different plans for the future.

I would therefore like to dedicate this book to my ex-boyfriend, without whom I may never have discovered my passion for sex positions. Which would mean that this book would never have been written. So: Felix, the first wheelbarrow with you was definitely the most exciting. Thank you for the good times! So, what happened next? Read for yourself!

Part 1

Pole Position: Getting Ready for Sex Positions

▼ From Kama Sutra to Gayma Sutra

Calling this book *Gayma Sutra* is a bit of a private joke. It's a nod to a personal desire I've held since puberty. As an adolescent, I used to jerk off to a couple of passages in the real *Kama Sutra*, but at the same time, I thought it was a shame that the hottest passages were always those about intercourse between a man and a woman. If you looked up oral sex, there was a chapter on sex between men, but that subject immediately veered off to the third sex and "secret desires," whose devotees had to disguise themselves as masseurs. Anal sex was only referred to in passing. So for a long time, I dreamed of publishing a gay version of the great "book of love" of Sanskrit literature. To be clear: this is not that book. There is too much emphasis on sex positions here for that, which, despite what you might have heard, is not actually the main focus of the real *Kama Sutra*, consisting as it does mainly of long-winded chapters on courtesans, courtship, and "seducing another man's wife" that you can't really adapt to a gay perspective—not that you'd want to.

I'll still be invoking some aspects of the original version and translating some of the positions from vaginal to anal intercourse. For one, becouse it would be a shame not to tell you about some of the peculiar disciplines such as the "bull's thrust," the "spinning top," or the "yawning position," and for another, because the underlying idea of the *Kama Sutra* is closely related to my motivation for this book. Both are about having pleasurable, creative, and uninhibited sex and enriching yourself and your partner by doing so. This is an aspect that, considering how old the *Kama Sutra* writings are (after all, they were written over 1,700 years ago), I still find remarkable. Obviously, the text was written against the background of the Indian caste system and affirms a heterosexual patriarchy, but underneath the mass of rituals, there is a relaxed liberal spirit that urges its followers to observe the balance between both sex partners. This aspect also plays an important role when you try out the positions.

Additionally, the *Kama Sutra* is a rejection of "weak" and "false" feelings and makes a case for "spontaneous" (i.e. deeply and unrestrainedly felt) love. According to the original version, you can succumb to the latter by courting the object of your desires with all sixty-four arts of the *Kama Sutra*. These do not, as frequently claimed, consist of sixty-four sex positions, but rather range from dance and song to intimate hygiene and are therefore simply ways of preparing for physical congress. Once this is achieved, the text turns pragmatic. Lube, dildos, role-play—it's all there in the *Kama Sutra*. Today's sexual mores are merely a reinterpretation of historic models.

▼ Sexual Compatibility: A Quick Test

There is an impressive passage in the *Kama Sutra* concerning penis size and hole depth—that is to say with the dimensions of your "lingam" (schlong) or "yoni" (vajayjay). Thus, a gentleman with an S-sized winkle would go in the "hare" category, while size M is a "bull," and anything over an L is "stallion." Sounds just like Grindr, doesn't it? But there's one thing that's always neglected in online dating, and that's the yoni category. In a gay context, you could easily turn that into the stretching capacity of your anus. Whether you really need to use the *Kama Sutra* categories "doe" (S), "mare" (M), or "female elephant" (L) is another matter, but calculating two partners' sexual compatibility based on matching these categories is worth a thought. This follows the simple principle of "birds of a feather flock together." So the "ideal matches" are hare-doe, bull-mare, and stallion-elephant. The others are "high" or "low" and "highest" and "lowest" matches, the "highest" match being stuffing an L-sized dick into an S-sized hole and the "lowest" would be inserting an S-sized dick into an L-sized hole.

These are the basics. I know a lot of you will be sitting, slack-jawed in disbelief, exclaiming either "Excuse me?" or "Bullshit!" I can fully comprehend both reactions. So let's clarify this with a visual presentation, and then we can proceed with the arguments behind this portentous test.

dick size   *hole size*

In a totally dick-fixated gay scene, digressions on penis size are often met with reactions that range from oversensitive to downright bitchy. For a more relaxed outlook on the topic you need to be both completely content with your own privates and able to transcend the mire of gay clichés. But who can lay claim to either quality? Speaking of the compatibility test, I have to admit that during puberty, it was a real turn-on for me. It was all about penis size. At the time, that was enough to get me worked up. But I was inevitably provoked by my recent rediscovery of the lingam-yoni-model. Re-reading the *Kama Sutra* after over a decade of gay socialization, these theories of the "ideal," "highest," and "lowest" combinations of physical attributes seemed merely crude, macho generalizations. It was only to be expected that shoving a gigantic dick into a tiny bajingo would be rated the "highest," while a mini-wang in a mega-hole was dismissed offhand as the "lowest match." This seemed to be the usual glorification of the insertive partner, with the concurrent denigration of the receptive role. And the "ideal" matches? Well, they were just more conservative bullshit, prioritizing normative behavior over breaking with conventions.

But soon enough, my theoretical indignation came into conflict with reflections on my own practical experience. In my early slutty phase, just after coming out, there was a time when I was obsessed with big dicks, but rarely could I live up to them in my role as a bottom. It was a classic example of one's eyes being bigger than one's hole. My uninitiated behind simply wasn't ready for the big guns yet. Conversely, later on, I experienced situations where I was confronted with extremely baggy fisting enthusiasts, who, to put it bluntly, made me feel like I was dipping my hard-on into rice pudding. I'm not saying that either situation would preclude any kind of rewarding experience for either participant, but it does require a certain measure of experience and flexibility. So neither situation is really "ideal" for an intense first hookup—and after all, the first phase of getting to know one another sexually is essentially what the *Kama Sutra* is all about.

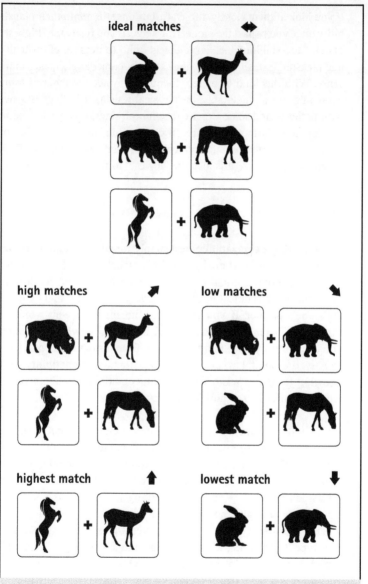

Matches

If you look at them closely, these attributions still retain their plausibility once you're past the pioneering stage. If you relate the "highest" match "doe-stallion" (i.e., large meets tight) to degrees of difficulty and pleasure instead of status, the category immediately makes more sense. With this kind of match, there are physical boundaries to be overcome and so, inevitably, the physical resistance is "highest," but with patience and some experience on both sides, it can also lead to the "highest" form of pleasure. In comparison, the combination of micro-penis meets rosebud creates the "lowest" resistance, but from an erotic perspective it is also the "lowest" form of stimulation.

▼ The Satisfaction Principle: Knowing, Saying, Doing

So let us see the compatibility test simply for what it ought to be: an unpretentious orientational guide. This model should be an aid for quickly assessing a situation, defining expectations and delineating one's sphere of action. All this can be very helpful to safely engage with one's partner. If you can gauge the situation, you won't be thrown off-balance that easily. And if you know what you want, you can protect yourself and your lover from disappointment. That's exactly the point I want to address with this compatibility test: knowing what you want. This is an unconditional requirement for enjoying different sex positions.

It's a bit like the whole top-bottom thing. I'm not a big fan of rigidly defined roles or the establishment of inflexible sexual functions. I also think that, in this age of online dating, we've taken the concept of pre-packaging our own needs too far. On the other hand, if you're on a spontaneous sex date with a stranger, it simply is necessary, otherwise you might end up with one of those ridiculous situations where "versatile" type A has his non-versatile sights set on "versatile" type B's backside, while at the same time you've got "versatile" type B trying to point his cannon at A's stern. It gets even more fraught if you have two sockets trying to connect.

I'm sure at least half of you have encountered a similar situation. I advise the others to spare themselves the misery and to adopt the motto: first know what you want, then say what you want, then do want you want! Subject to your partner's consent, of course. In the best case, this motto should work in the plural anyway, but if at least one partner (that would be you) follows it, then you're halfway there. After all, there are some less decisive people out there who need another person to indicate their intentions in order to identify their own needs. But that's high-grade psychology and doesn't really belong here. Instead, let's put our orientation guide to good use and train our willpower with this key to the positions.

▶ Key to Positions

Sorry, but this isn't a secret and magical shortcut to mastering every conceivable sex position. This "key" is merely a set of symbols I'll be using to refine the following medley of positions for better orientation—like the key to a map. As we can apply the high-/low- ideal categories from our compatibility model on a nearly one-to-one basis to the difficulty and potential for satisfaction of every sex position, the lessons in this book will also be tagged according to our established arrow system.

 = Complicated, but ... I'm cumming!

 = Sex fitness at its best

 = Not original, but pretty hot

 = Contortionist's pleasure

 = Olympics, not orgasms

Key to Positions

While trying out these positions, I also noticed that some positions are more suited to certain moods and occasions than others. If you just want to get your hump on, you might not appreciate the romantic qualities of a love swing. Conversely, you won't want to switch to pile driver mode if you're in the mood for a cuddle. So in addition to the arrow symbol, I've tagged each position with an appropriate mood label. Sounds a bit gimmicky, but it's actually quite useful. I'll explain why with this personal anecdote: in preparation for writing this book, I bought myself a notebook where I collected suggestions made by friends and fuck buddies as well as interesting positions I'd stumbled upon in pornos and darkrooms. Pretty soon I had a whole heap of ideas I was planning on consulting, when my date turned up at my door. So do you think that, in spite of the wealth of notes

 Barbell = For fitness fetishists. A workout that happens to include sex.

Clock = Spontaneous, fast, and sexy. The ideal quickie!

 Heart = The romantic touch! If you're not in love yet, you will be after this position.

Poppers = Orgies and poppers. The perfect position for a marathon fuck.

 Dice = Hot, sexy fun. Games for big boys.

Mood labels

and sketches at my disposal, I was able to find even one position that corresponded to my mood? Nope. Frantically searching for tips for a quickie, all I could find was yoga sex and complicated contortionist moves. I wound up doing exactly the opposite of what I was supposed to do to follow the satisfaction principle formulated earlier on: I was confused, and for the entire date, I wasn't sure of what I wanted. I've completely forgotten what we did then, but it certainly didn't merit a new entry in my notebook. After that, I began to add symbols to my notes. For a while I must have had a dozen of them. Far too many. These five mood standards are quite enough.

That covers mood and degrees of difficulty, but all sexy things come in threes. So last but not least, I've turned to the table of contents of *69 Positions of Joyful Gay Sex*. When we were working on this book, we gave each position a little box for the readers to check off once they had tried it out. It was a nice way of encouraging readers to join in, and I'd like to pass it on to the readers of the *Gayma Sutra*. So that's why I've put empty boxes in this book as well, which you will hopefully be able to check off soon. Cum and check off! You can use the picture below to practice! And I came up with another gimmick for some rest and recreation in between positions. There's some bonus material included at the end of this book, a set of "Game-A-Sutra" cards for you to cut out. You can play this game with your partner and find out more about the principle behind the compatibility test. See page 75 for how to play. And now it's time to have a look at what the pros are doing.

Autofellatio: A piece of cake for well-endowed Scott O'Hara

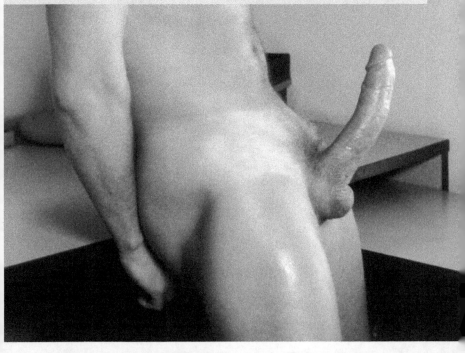

What the Pros Are Doing:
Key Positions from Scott O'Hara to Davey Wavey

To get you in the mood, it can't hurt to pick up a few tips from the experts. There are any number of porn celebrities around in the gay scene to provide you with a couple of ideas for your bedtime acrobatics. But not all of our position pros are from the sex film sector. There's someone here—from savant to clown—for everyone. So, it's curtain up for the top ten position stars.

▼ Scott O'Hara: Autofellatio

A man answering to the great nickname "Spunk" and packing an eleven-inch schlong is for all intents and purposes predestined for experimentation. Scott O'Hara fit this bill by first being awarded the title of "Man With the Biggest Dick in San Francisco" in the early eighties and then going on to distinguish himself by becoming the King of autofellatio. This term is a compound of the Latin "auto" (self) and "fellare," "to suck." In plain English, this means nothing other than "sucking yourself off." Statistically, only around two to three percent of the male population worldwide are capable of performing this feat of masturbation on themselves. In my personal opinion, there could be more, but most gentlemen simply lose interest in contorting themselves for the sake of a brotherly kiss with their own bellends once they have had a couple of sexual encounters with a partner. Which is why autofellatio will remain a privilege reserved for a few outstandingly well-endowed boys. For while the average gay man has to perform half a somersault backwards or at least lean on a wall and press his ass downwards in order to suck his own genitals, all a power pecker like Scott O'Hara has to do is bend his back and lower his head. In 1992, as part of his project on *Sexual Art*, American photographer Michael A. Rosen shot an impressive photo of Scott doing what he did best. In the age of AIDS, autofellatio was often jokingly referred to as the ultimate safe sex practice.

But it wasn't enough, even for a real artist, as the case of Scott O'Hara proves: He died of AIDS-related complications in February 1998, aged only 37, after a short but vivid life spent as an icon of porn, punk, and poetry.

▼ Marc Dylan: Doggy Style

Some of the classic moves are just as popular among the pros. If you ask around among professional porn bottoms what their personal favorite position is, seventy percent of them will tell you it's "doggy style." It's easy to see why. Veteran bottoms love the element of surprise and the focus on pure sensation that characterize

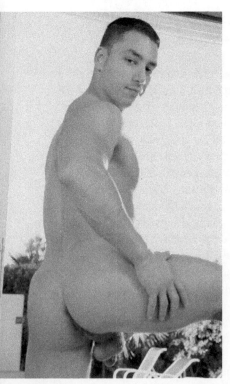

this position. With the receptive partner crouching on all fours like a dog and being pounded from behind, he can only make eye-contact by glancing, if at all, over his shoulder. This leaves him free to focus on the hot sensations going on in his ass and to reduce communications with his partner to barking verbal demands and sticking out his rear end invitingly. Everything else is a kind of surrender, which is what gives true passivity its extra spice. Doggy style is a very stable position, so there isn't much you can do wrong. Supremely jacked sex star Marc Dylan, who performs this classic move in countless professional scenes, but also in private, provides us with the valuable gourmet tip: "Best way to do doggy: bottom at the edge of the bed," the American stud tells *Male Star Blog*, "ass up, face down, the top standing up behind him (...) feels so amazing!" And he's right. It gives the expression "nailing someone to the mattress" an entirely new quality.

▼ Big Dipper: Big Dipper

This Chicago-based rapper and big gay bear is into face-to-face sex, because eye contact is what turns him on. At first glance, his name, whether in the sense of the constellation Ursa Major, or the roller coaster, would seem to have nothing to do with this. But for those in the know, the "Big Dipper" is also a sex position—one that

combines eye contact with an athletic bonus: with your back to the couch, supporting yourself with both hands on the edge, you place both feet on a stool in front of you, creating a bridge between the two pieces of furniture with your body. Then have your naked partner stand astride you and insert bridge guy's (your) boner into his butt. Now thrust. Sexual friction can be created in this position only by having the top thrust into his partner's hole from below by doing a reverse push-up, or the guy on the receiving end rhythmically flexing his knees. The man on top gets a pretty decent thigh workout, with the guy on the bottom working on his abs and arm muscles. It's great for all you gym bunnies out there, hell for the couch potatoes,

and on top of that, a very nice way to re-discover the joys of taking it slow. Instead of increasing the pace of your thrusts (as you generally do during sex), the big dipper will tire you out and slow you down. Has the Chicago rapper experienced the same thing? I asked him and he told me: "Never heard of it, but I'll try it out and see if my arms can take it." That's the spirit. In any case, the songs on Big Dipper's debut album *Thick Life* are an appropriately frenetic accompaniment to this discipline.

▼ Paul Stag: The Pile Driver

Grabby Award-winner and leather escort Paul Stag likes to play hard and rough and swears by the pile driver position. The name says it all, really: the bottom lies head down on the ground with his legs spread wide or thrown back over his head, while the top rams his

piston straight down into his lucky partner's hole. Just like a pile driver. An important aspect of this position is that it allows for very deep penetration and there is little the bottom can do to counter the top's pounding. So power play is an integral part of this position. Just the thing for military fetishist Paul Stag. "The pile driver is a speciality of mine," he tells *QXMen* magazine, "as I like to own and destroy an ass and see all the pain and desire in a guy's eyes." Paul Stag's belligerent tone speaks volumes. His favorite position is not the safest method around, as a too impetuous pounding from the top may sprain or even fracture the bottom's neck.

▼ Jessie Colter: The Cowboy

Kentucky-based bottom Jessie Colter stays true to his cowboy roots—even during sex: "I like to ride a guy! Problem is I can't last very long in that position ... if you know what I mean." Of course we know what he means. Anyone who has ever had his partner lie flat on his back, straddled his dick in the cowboy position and then purposefully galloped off into an orgasmic sunset, will know how easy it is to climax quickly in this position. You just get carried away. Unlike most other positions, the guy being penetrated is almost entirely in control in this position. He determines the depth, rhythm and angle of his ride, all the stallion on the bottom can do is thrust a bit harder. Congratulations to all of you with great control over your sphincter muscles, you can use those to massage your partner's prick. This is also one of power bottom Jessie Colter's specialties: "I can milk a cock with the most perfect rhythm using nothing more than my ass muscles. I don't even have to move anything else." You can watch a sample of this cute American's riding skills in the Lucas Entertainment production *Men in Love* and watch him put dark Venezuelan stallion Jean Franko through his paces.

▼ Jake Bass: Missionary Position

This one has the rather dubious reputation of being the favorite position of boring straight couples. So who would have thought that inked-up CockyBoy Jake Bass of all people would be into missionary? OK, so that would be everyone who gets off on sex that's intimate as well as intense. This position guarantees both intimacy and intensity for the top and the bottom in equal measure. Both partners get to feel especially close in this position, where the bottom lies on his back with his legs apart and raised, while his partner mounts him. Jake Bass has had tons of experience in this position, both topping and bottoming, and knows how to appreciate the missionary position. "I'm a very passionate young man," he confesses to online magazine *Gayletter*, "eye contact and lips at reach are a must.."

Jake Bass (right) with CockyBoys colleague Asher Hawk

▼ Trey Turner: The Bridge BJ

The most adorable squint in porno is so fixated on cocks that during a FalconExclusive date with Dylan Roberts, he never got past the oral phase, and Lucas Entertainment's model catalogue introduces him with the byline: "It's all about blow jobs when Trey Turner is concerned: it's his favorite thing to do sexually, and when he's performing in front of the camera, it's clear he's got amazing skill with his mouth and tongue!" These words seem to have acted as an incentive for the modest Floridian to aspire to higher things. While shooting for Dominic Ford's 3D studio, he proved that blow jobs are not limited to one's mouth and tongue, but that you can use your entire body. During foreplay with Shane Frost, he delighted his audience not only with his famous deep-throat panting, he also performed a bridge (a gymnastics exercise that involves both hands and feet on the ground while you arch your back, creating a curve with your body) and sucked his co-star's hard-on upside down. A spectular sight, unmistakably demonstrating his rank as king of sex positions. Especially as Turner kept his rock-hard boner the entire time. Respect!

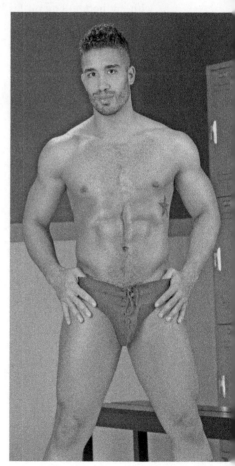

▼ Tom Wolfe: The Leg-Lock

Juicy porn star Tom Wolfe is a dyed-in-the-wool top and has developed his own method of taking possession of his sex partners. He literally performs a leg-lock on them. In an interview with GayDemon.com, he explains how to do this in so much detail that we can only do justice to his description by quoting the original: "I love to drive it deep and hard! My all-time favorite position is with my bottom boy on his back so I can see his eyes and watch

his face as I pleasure his tight hole. I want his hips twisted to his left as I straddle his left leg and his right leg over my left shoulder. This allows me to fuck like an animal, penetrating deep and hard, with my right arm able to reach under him and help support his lower back, giving it the desirable arch. While my left arm holds him in place and tightly to my body, just in case I get one that tries to squirm away." Hear, hear. Tom Wolfe's fuck-lock is a real exercise in multitasking. It's probably a bit too contorted to be really appreciated by porn directors, but you can get at least an impression of the Wolfe-Man's favorite position in a scene with Angelo Marconi in the Raging Stallion movie *Suited for Sex.*

▼ Davey Wavey: Bus Driver, Darth Vader, Banana Split

In his two-and-a-half minute YouTube video *Creative Sex Positions*, gay superblogger Davey Wavey airs his complaints about the way gay porn videos always seem to follow the same plot. "Sex is supposed to be fun and exciting and creative," he says, "and none of that is really captured by porn."

Our look at what positions the pros have been doing would seem to contradict this view, but as Davey Wavey follows up his criticism with a very constructive crash course on sex positions, I won't keep the top three positions in his alternative porn program from you—these being the "bus driver," "Darth Vader," and the "banana split."

The professor has a couple of cute interns demonstrate the first two, and joins in himself for the last. I have taken the liberty of working out the following Davey-Wavey-Preference-Charts:

- **Third Place: The Bus Driver**
  The "vehicle" lies on his back with his knees bent while the "driver" puts the fingers of his left hand into his rectum and moves them from side to side, essentially driving the bus. At the same time, he grabs his partner's "horn" (chest) with his right hand, squeezing until he "honks." Drive safely!

- **Second Place: Darth Vader**
  This galactic game is more of a role-play than a sexual position, but by limiting your breathing capacity, constraining your view, and making a great, booming sound, it is guaranteed to promote your sensual awareness. You know what's coming: for this stunt, the extra kick is supplied by the eponymous rubber mask (you can buy a costume of the *Star Wars* villain at any comic store). It's not as childish as it sounds. Sex with masks is always a game of skill and can contribute to a heightened arousal of your desire sensors. I'll come back to this topic later. For the moment, I would suggest that cosplay newcomers do a trial run with the somewhat cheaper blindfold.

- **First Place: Banana Split**
  A sweet and sticky pleasure. Sweet-toothed Davey lies on his back naked while his upper body is garnished with cream, sprinkles and hot fudge. After that, his personal kitchen boys pull his legs apart and shove the "banana" up his ass. Again, more on this later ...

▼ Dolph & Kris: The New 69ers

Dolph Lambert and Kris Evans from the Slovakian porn label Bel Ami won't be labeled. Not by their sexual preferences, nor according to a certain male type, or even by a specific position. There are two reasons why I had to include them here anyway: for one, their participation in the book *69 Positions of Joyful Gay Sex* has made them the official ambassadors of the 69 position, for another, they will be contributing to this book as well and demonstrating all kinds of positions. Which is why a brief introduction seems appropriate. Dark-haired Kris is a pin up boy as well as the poster boy for the ranks of Bel Ami's models. This Hungarian cutie lost his position in the police force in 2010 due to his porn activities. Since then, he has been working full-time for Bel Ami, where he generally plays the top. His versatile blond colleague Dolph is equally happy to top or

bottom. He is another of the Bel Ami label's long time favorites, and also works for them as a coordinator and unit manager. Dolph grew up on a farm in the Czech Republic and studied IT. He made international headlines in the summer of 2012 by holidaying on the beaches of St. Tropez with none other than Elton John. With their *69 Positions*, Dolph and Kris have set new trends in their sex scenes together, whether with two or three people or in a group. In short: with reference to the peace movement of the 1960s, I would like to nominate these two as official representatives of the new 69ers of sex positions. And now, we've seen enough. Before we go on to fill our heads with more information, we need to clear them first.

Save and turn the page!

Free Your Mind—and Drop Your Pants!
Getting Your Mind and Body into Position

▼ Free Your Mind: Four Types, One Common Denominator

Right, now we know what the stars are into. This leads us to the question: what does this mean for us? It's no coincidence that I placed the chapter on what the pros are doing before the main part of this book. The reason for this is easily explained. I gave the last chapter to some friends to read through and asked for their feedback. The reactions I got differed wildly. Some of them thought it was all really boring and said they didn't need porn stars to explain their sex lives to them. I'll call this group the "know-it-alls." Then there were those who were primarily concerned with the more conventional positions such as missionary and doggy style and were surprised or pleased to find out that sex workers were pretty much the same as everyone else—I'll call them the "normals." Last but not least, there were those who immediately honed in on points such as the pile driver, Darth Vader, or the blow job bridge and started discussing those—along the lines of "no one does that anyway" or "that's just showing off." I've called this group "intimidated."

I'm just going to assume that every reader will at least in part see himself in one or another of these groups and so I'd like to ask you to not misconstrue my categories as any kind of judgment. I merely derived them from what I knew or assumed I knew about their respective members' sex lives.

By which I mean that the know-it-alls were generally people with a wealth of experience in dating and sex clubs, resulting in a pragmatic view of their own sexuality, which in itself made them particularly resistant to advice. They've done a lot, seen a lot, and are hard to impress. Jaded and egocentric also spring to mind.

The normals on the other hand were people whose sexual behavior were more domestic, frequently couples living according to monogamous ideals. To them, the inclusion of predicable standard positions confirmed their own, more conventional, views on sexuality.

I would describe the intimidated group as people wrestling with their own lack of experience, who perceived anything that overstepped the boundaries of their own personal experiences as a threat.

All of these viewpoints are understandable and legitimate, but they all lack the one thing I would see as a key requirement when reading this book: curiosity. If you're going to have the courage to try out new positions it is absolutely essential that you do not view sex as a performance, nor as a necessary evil. After all, accidents do happen. In these cases, you need to be able to laugh at yourself and just try out something else, without seeing yourself as a failure—or being afraid of the other guy seeing you that way. Part of that is allowing for sexual moods. You won't always be in the same mood and enjoying one position the first time does not guarantee you will enjoy it as much a second time, or with another guy. The same goes for the reverse.

On this basis, I would have preferred to have had more feedback along the lines of "Wow, will the big dipper build up my biceps?" or "Pelvis on the left and legs over the left shoulder? At first I thought some porn dummy must have gotten the sides wrong, but the leg-lock really does work." Or fine, even something like "Next time my boyfriend's horny and I'm not in the mood, I'll just 'drive his bus'."

I did get some of these reactions, and so they form a fourth category: "open-minded." And that is how we should all start out with the practical part of this book. The open-minded group do not immediately hone in on what they already know, what they reject, or what they can't do, rather they focus on stuff that seems new or possibly fun. The great thing about this is that trying out predefined positions can often lead to discovering completely new ones. I'll add some of my own suggestions later on, these being, so to speak, my personal inventions. I mean to say, I didn't research and test them, I simply ended up with them while trying out other positions. "Leapfrog" is of these positions. So is "Boccie Balls." But I'm getting ahead of myself here. What I mean is: just use this book as a springboard to bounce your own sexual creativity off. And when I say use, that's exactly what I mean. Let's start right now.

▼ Drop Your Pants–The Gayma Sutra Initiation

The point of any book is that it has to be read in order to fulfill its function. The *Gayma Sutra* is no exception. However, I do not want you to treat this book with the exaggerated amount of respect awarded to literary works by many of their readers. I don't want you to simply read this book, I expressly want you to use it. Who cares if the pages get crumpled or torn if you haven't managed to set it aside in the heat of the moment. Or if you leave lube prints on its pages. Or if you scribble the names of those sex partners the respective positions went especially well with in the margins. To put it bluntly, you could say that the *Gayma Sutra* will only have fulfilled its purpose once it carries these traces of use.

Now I am aware from my own experience that your brain is not a flash drive you can just load a new relaxation and value program onto that will make everything nice and easy. You can't just shrug off years of carefully cultivated habits and deeply engrained conventions at the drop of a hat. But I do know that it can be helpful to be specifically told to overstep ones's own self-imposed boundaries. I've got a great, even kind of cultured example for this.

A couple of years ago, I was hanging out at the Swiss art fair in Basel and came across a niche with a large mirror standing in it at an angle, soiled with dirty, partly dried streaks, and with a sign above it that read "spit on me." It was pretty early in the morning and clearly no one had complied with this request yet that day. But the streaks meant that people had done so at some point previously. At that moment, I was overcome by a peculiar combination of inhibitedness and a sense of obligation. I was inhibited because I was not brought up to expectorate in an enclosed space and in full public view. The sense of obligation was because I thought to myself, "First of all, it would be cowardly not to obey this order, even though you're tempted to. Secondly, if you don't do it, you will only confirm the artist's assumptions of a rigidly conventional society which presumably formed the basis of this work. Thirdly, if you don't have a problem with fulfilling the requests of sex partners who want to be spat at, then what's your problem with spitting at a damn mirror, just because because it's standing around at a swanky art fair." To put it briefly: I spat at it—and the next moment I realized I had just gobbed a load of spit at myself, because of course the mirror was angled so that it reflected your face back at you while you spat. So the whole thing kind of backfired on me there. But the more important thing for me was feeling that I had overcome my own inhibitions. Apart from that: I don't have a problem with being spat at occasionally during sex, so I'm not going to start developing feelings of disgust if I do it to myself. So I chalked the entire thing up to experimentation and went on my way.

Getting back to my original topic: to make it easier for you to use this book without any inhibitions, I've come up with this small initiation rite. It's also a kind of desecration rite too, if you like. So, to underscore the interactive qualities of this book at the outset, this is your first exercise:

Jerk off onto the next page! I promise you won't damage the paper and it won't get streaky or start to smell. I've tested that as well. Just make sure the page doesn't stick to the other pages; leave it open until it dries. The timing's good. After all, you deserve a break after the Gayma Sutra mind-opening ritual. Then we'll proceed to the sex gym!

Your turn to cum!

The Sex Gym: Build Up Your Gay Sex Muscles

There are two types of sex muscles: the ones directly involved in the act and others that have a different function originally, but still play an important part during sex. In this chapter we will be working on both types. Plus a couple more things that have less to do with strength and more to do with sex drive. My goal here isn't primarily to strengthen the respective muscle groups but rather to increase awareness of how they function. If you are aware of your body's centers of strength, then you can target them specifically—a supremely useful ability to have for a position marathon.

Knowing your body has other advantages too: you can build up your muscles as part of your daily routine, without using weights or paying gym fees. Whether you're sitting in the waiting room, on your daily drive to work, standing in line for groceries ... in principle, you can upgrade your power packs the entire time. You just need to know where they are, how to flex them properly and what they're for. Tireless long-distance tops, for instance, should work on their abs, while dedicated bottom boys would be well advised to not only build up their butts, but in particular their legs as well. I'll be telling you why in this chapter.

I'm not saying I'm reinventing the wheel here, but perhaps I can fill a couple of gaps in your knowledge. Even your average Joe Six-Pack will occasionally encounter muscles of whose existence he had previously been unaware. These encounters generally take the form of aches or soreness. My personal awakening was the discovery of my musculus genioglossus, better know as the extrinsic tongue muscle.

I woke up one morning with a strange twinge in the area around my lower tongue. At first, it only hurt when I swallowed, but then it also became painful if I moved my tongue back and forth or stuck it out. Normally, this would have made me uneasy, but in this case the cause of my affliction was obvious. To be precise, he was lying naked next to me, butt raised enticingly, snoring to beat the band. I had hooked up with this guy at a bar the night before and he had initiated me into the art of rimming. Not consciously, of course. Ultimately, his ravenous desire to have his ass licked had simply piqued my ambition, so I had performed the tongue dance so excessively that my tongue muscles were now feeling the effects. Not a bad way to find out more about the miracle of the human body—and for me it was the reason why I still do tongue circling exercises for two minutes every morning after brushing my teeth. After all, you never know what's in store for you.

This last sentence sums up the main reason for our visit to the sex gym in a nutshell: you need to be prepared for all the stretch and strain that awaits you in the *Gayma Sutra*. And you need to be aware that good preparation does not necessarily mean a lot of effort or expensive equipment. Sometimes ten minutes in private per day are enough to increase your staying power, and a simple butt-plug may suffice to enhance your sphincter tolerance. So no excuses for slacking. And none are needed. The exercises here are so easy, our ten-point plan should leave even the lazybones among you eager for more. Once this is a given, the rest will take care of itself. As you know, physical activity increases the testosterone count in your blood, and with it, your sexual desire. So let's go!

▼ Exercise 1: The Penis Raise

You've all heard of the exercise where you hang a towel over your erect penis to test the strength of your erections. Most of you have probably tried it out and realized just how stubborn and unsexy a towel draped over your boner can feel—and how ridiculous it looks. I've revamped the basic principle and turned it into a game.

To do this, you'll need a jockstrap (a pair of briefs will do in a pinch), a couple of solid balls (such as boccie or billiard balls, a pair of baoding balls will do nicely) and a fully erect penis. Hang the jockstrap

Give me your billiard balls!
Hot House star Tyler Saint is all prepped for the penis raise

over your boner. The pouch where your junk usually goes should be dangling downwards. Then stand with your feet shoulder-width apart, and lower yourself down into a squat. Once you're in a squatting position, take the first ball and put it in the support pouch. Then straighten up again, pulling the weight up with you. Once you're upright, slowly count to ten. Then squat down again, add the second ball and repeat the exercise—until your dick can no longer hold the weights. This exercise will train your erectile discipline, your leg muscles, and your coordination.

Warning: the support pouch's limited capacity will generally keep you from taking this too far, but I still want to point out that the aim here is not to go on increasing the weight until you manage to "conquer" your boner, or even snap it off. That would not only be dangerous, but also really unsexy. So please, no bowling balls! To avoid any misunderstanding, I would also like to point out that your dick is not a muscle, nor does it consist of muscles. How hard your dick is depends simply on the blood flow to the erectile tissue. The duration of your erection depends on the concentration of its owner. This introductory exercise is designed to train the latter. That is what I mean by the term "erectile discpline."

If do you insist on doing justice to the title of this chapter by using the penis raise to stimulate your muscles, you can contract your pelvic floor to make your boner and the attached weights bounce. We'll be focusing on this principle in the second exercise.

A great variation on the penis raise for the more advanced is to use an additional testicle weight. You can easily make this yourself as well. Simply hitch a broad lanyard just above your balls (rock-climbers would call this a cow hitch) and attach a soda can (or even better, a swing-top bottle), filled with the desired amount of liquid to the ring. Don't overdo this either, but otherwise, enjoy the ball-stretch!

▼ Exercise 2: The Big Kegel

We briefly mentioned this in the first exercise, but now it's time to get down to the nitty-gritty. The famous pelvic floor exercises, also known as Kegel exercises after their inventor, the American gynecologist Arnold Kegel, are generally mentioned in the rather off-putting context of urinary incontinence. So if you have trouble with your waterworks, you might want to pay twice as much attention, and for the rest of you: "Kegels" stimulate not only the pubococcygeus muscle but also the so-called "love muscle" (ischiocavernosus muscle). The latter creates a pumping motion to transport blood into the erectile tissue of your penis during an erection. So if you can contract it at will, you will be able to influence your sexual stamina as well as the timing and intensity of your orgasms. So let's get started.

As these muscles are quite far inside your body, they are also known as "invisible muscles." Which means that, unlike, say, your biceps or calf muscles, you can barely see them contracting with the naked eye. Just barely. By lying down on your back naked in front of a mirror, your legs bent, and then taking a look at the seam between the end of your ball sac and your crack, you get a general idea of their whereabouts. If you then contract your pelvic muscles (as if you were trying not to pee or stopping your piss in midstream), the seam will bulge outwards slightly. If you don't have a mirror on hand, you can try

Time to get down!

feeling for it by placing your index finger on the place and feeling it swell whenever you tense your muscles. This is an unmistakable sign of the pelvic floor muscles contracting.

And that is really the entire secret of Kegel exercises. The first instruction is to "contract your pelvic floor" and the second is to "hold for as long as possible." You can do this anywhere really, but to do it properly you should take your time and try it out at home. That way you can focus on what your pelvic floor is doing and concentrate especially on your breathing. Otherwise you can get dizzy. I would advise this three-step program:

- First: Take off your clothes, stand in a relaxed pose, breathe deeply, and then contract your ass muscles as if you were trying to crack a walnut between them.

- Second: While keeping your butt tensed in walnut-cracking mode, do the aforementioned pee-barrier contraction. Squeeze as hard as possible.

- Third: Squat down like a ski-jumper and count until you can no longer hold the pelvic contraction. The tension should be confined to your pelvis—keep the rest of your body relaxed and breath slowly.

Repeat the exercise ten times while trying to hold the tension longer each time. One tip: this exercise is especially effective when done with a hard-on. Not necessarily because it works better, but because your motivation and control will be greater that way. In general, it has been scientifically proven that men have more strength and stamina during physical activities if they're horny. A randy athlete is a good athlete. Try doing the big Kegel with and without an erection, and see if you can confirm this theory.

Doing Kegels with an erection has the added effect of making your boner bounce up due to the contraction of your pelvic floor. This not only enhances pleasure, it is also a sign that you are doing it right.

You can do a complementary exercise to the big Kegel that acts as a balance. This is important and necessary to attain the desired effect. So if you want to get started right away, please check out the "Counterstrike" in exercise six first.

▼ Exercise 3: The Male Quadriga

The quadriga is an ancient Greek or Roman chariot drawn by four horses, as depicted on the Brandenburg Gate in Berlin or the Wellington Arch in London. In most of the bronze sculptures around the world, this historical vehicle is usually driven by women, so it is high time we had a few male quadrigas to revive this antiquated motif for the *Gayma Sutra* age. Therefore, I would propose this motto for the following exercise: thigh muscles, not horse power.

We will be training our quadriceps. This is the large muscle group on the front of your thighs that acts as an extensor for your knee joint. As the name suggests, it is made up of four large muscles. As none of the standing sex positions would be possible without your quads, they are an important part of a varied sex life. Once I realized this, I spent some time doing a great many squats. This was quite effective in itself and I would never advise against it, but to be quite honest with you, I got pretty bored with it after a while. And so I switched to the following bodybuilding exercise: deadlifts.

Fittingly enough, it was a fuck buddy who pointed me towards this exercise. This guy was really into fitness. A tad too much into it for my taste, he seemed to prefer handling his dumbbells to handling my dick. To me, this guy never managed to strike the balance between arousing desire and satisfying these desires. To put it bluntly, his beautiful body was a real turn-on, but after the first round he'd always had enough, and instead of indulging in sexual excesses, he preferred to go on tedious digressions on how his training was going. Unsatisfying in the long run, but for a while we found a compromise in voyeurism, i.e., having him perform his exercises for me. I can't recall most of them, but I did remember the deadlifts—this can be attributed to my basic instincts. This exercise consists of standing with your feet apart and lifting a barbell with your arms stretched and your back straight, so that all the effort comes from your rear end and thighs. This means that you have to stick your ass out when raising and lowering the weight, which really looked exceptionally sexy when my fuck-buddy did it. If you try googling images for "deadlifts," you'll form your own opinions on how much of an acceptable and pragmatic alternative my personal interpretation is. As I am not in possession of a barbell, I tried applying the same principle using a crate of beer. That worked well, and still does. The term "quadriceps" eventually led me to give the exercise the silly name I've used in this book. If you pause while squatting low, you really can feel like you're driving a quadriga, with the reins in your hands. Perhaps only once you've helped yourself to a couple of beers from the crate, but all the same.

And this leads us to a very important point: whatever utensil you use for your own personal quadriga, please always make sure that it isn't too heavy and that you keep your back straight while lifting, otherwise you could seriously injure yourself. And having sex in a standing position with a back injury is no fun at all, no matter how strong your thighs are.

One more thing: if my reference to standing positions immediately calls to mind a beefy stud pounding his lover, you wouldn't be wrong, but you are forgetting about the other side. As I've said before, bottom boys would be especially well advised to work on building up powerful leg muscles. I don't have to tell the adepts of this discipline that the innumerable variations on spreading your legs, which we will be discussing later on, can put a real strain on your leg muscles. So I highly recommend deadlifts to bottoms in particular. The pause position, held in the manner of a quadriga driver, with your back arched and your butt sticking out, speaks for itself.

▼ Exercise 4: The Taming of the Shrew

After these three physical exercises it is now time for a short lesson in pyschology. If you want to control the timing of your sexual climax and would like it to be more intense, you need to learn to regulate it. We'll be practicing this, too, in our sex gym. Basically, an orgasm is like a wild animal. You have to tame it before it will obey you. There is an abundance of methods out there aimed at domesticating your lust with names like "stop and go," "edging," or "ballooning," but essentially they all rely on the same technique: preventing ejaculation. This is to prevent those awkward moments when, consumed by the fire of passion, you thrust just one more time, even though you know you shouldn't if you want to continue. The magic words are "orgasm control"—and above all this involves mental work.

Speaking for myself, I have grown to appreciate the "teasing and denial" method, especially while trying out sex positions. It can be incredibly annoying to spend the entire evening looking forward to the "profound" experience of a "fuckquake," only to have your dam bust while you're still in shallow waters. And annoyance has no place in the *Gayma Sutra*, so we'll spend a bit of our time exercising restraint.

This is how it works: set a timer to twenty minutes and start jacking off. Your goal is now to postpone ejaculation until the time is up, while keeping your erection the entire time. Twenty minutes is quite enough time to reach a sensual climax, during which you need to suppress ejaculation. You can deploy the squeeze technique (use two fingers to firmly squeeze the shaft of your penis just below the glans) or the Kegel techniques from our second exercise, but the best strategy is to be aware of your body's own signals and to stop flogging your log in time. For masochists, this method of playing with your own boundaries is the supreme discipline, for everyone else, it's a lesson in humility towards the forces of your own desire. Either way, after twenty minutes you will be rewarded by an especially explosive climax.

Before trying out your newly found control with other people, you should undertake this procedure every two days at least for about two weeks. If you're in a relationship, you can do the countdown with your boyfriend. Practicing with a partner generally means the sensation is a lot more pleasurable than if you're on your own, and so it's a far greater challenge. If that still isn't enough for you, you may want to try "ballooning." This extreme variation on the teasing and denial theme completely omits the release of ejaculating. Instead, your goal is to learn how to experience dry (and multiple!) orgasms. I freely admit that I have not mastered this high art and that the only time I ever experienced a dry orgasm, it was due to a depletion of my semen resources. Presumably that doesn't count and, as it doesn't play a role in this book, I'm going to leave this one to the experts.

▼ Exercise 5: Deep Throat

We'll be embarking on exercise number five with the battle cry "deep throat!" Our goal is the high, or should we say highest form of fellatio: to swallow an erect male penis in its entirety. The bad news here is that even "realistic" dildos aren't much use for practicing this art form. The good news is that a real dick is significantly easier to swallow than a stinking lump of penis-shaped plastic—the human organ is a lot more supple than any replica could ever be. But that doesn't mean that deep throating with a real sex partner is a walk in the park. The path to the ultimate gullet job is strewn with tears and

discomfiture. No one has ever mastered this skill on the first attempt. Ultimately, only regular practice on a living subject makes perfect. But there are still a couple of tips I can give you.

- **Hang in there:** for a real blow-job artist the challenge is to suppress or rather control your gag reflex, which is triggered by the glans entering the pharynx. The important thing here is not to recoil on the first attempt, but to keep up the tension. When you're at the point of gagging, keep the dick in your mouth for as long as possible, swallow and breathe through your nose. Then "spit it out" and repeat the exercise. The second time around you'll notice that you are much better able to assess your own gag reflex and that you already have more control over it. This will help you later, when you try to move past it.

- **Position:** how difficult it is to advance into your throat depends not only on the blower's abilities, but also on the shape of the blowee's penis. For instance, a hard-on that curves upwards is best engulfed upside down. That way, you adapt the curve of the penis to the anatomy of your throat, which dips down steeply behind your tongue.

- **Technique:** once you have learned how to control your gag reflex, you can progress to the top discipline: sucking the glans into your throat. In addition to your partner's thrusts, it is especially helpful to use your tongue here. Try to push your tongue forwards along his dick as if you were going to stick it out. And when you pull it back again, suck his boner a little further back into your throat.

- **Breathing:** as a rule, it is important not to forget your breathing when you're sucking somebody off, but you need to breathe properly. This means that you should, contrary to popular belief, keep your breathing shallow and under no circumstances take a deep breath before the dick's descent. This will narrow your throat and increase the risk of the glans getting stuck. In general, don't forget to breathe through your nose!

▼ Exercise 6: The Big Kegel—the Counterstrike

Contraction should always be followed by relaxation. This rule applies to sex in general, but to the sex gym in particular. So we'll follow up on the teeth-clenching big Kegel exercise with the reverse Kegel. This is related to exercise 2 not only in name—the two should be performed as a combo for best results. Vigorous one-sided Kegels can cause cramps in your pelvic floor. This is more of a hindrance to controlling your love muscle than a help. So please make sure to balance out the number of times you do the Kegel and the reverse Kegel.

Now for the practical part: while the challenge in exercise 2 consisted of clenching your buttocks and closing off your pee barrier, the counterstrike involves doing the exact opposite. You could call it puffing up your pelvis. Where previously we had made use of the mechanisms controlling urination, this time we will be simulating pushing out a strong stream of piss. This sort of feels as if you were puffing up the front of your pelvis from the inside, which is why this exercise is also known as the "front reverse Kegel." The second component is the "back reverse Kegel." As the name would suggest, the focus here is on puffing out your backside, i.e., pushing out your asshole. I don't think I need to tell you that it's not a good idea to try this out if you really need to pee or fart. Here's the whole thing in three easy steps:

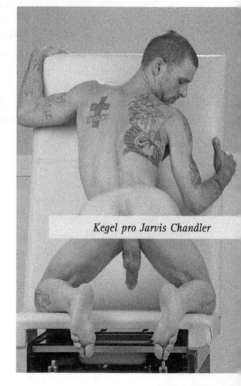

Kegel pro Jarvis Chandler

- **First:** Take off your clothes, stand in a relaxed position, take a deep breath and distend your sphincter outwards into a "back reverse Kegel." I've deliberately not use the word "press" here, as this exercise should not be performed using brute force.

- **Second:** Leaving your backside distended, send in reinforcements from the front, meaning add a "front reverse Kegel." At first, most people intuitively do both variations at the same time. But for proper control, you should do each of them separately.

- **Third:** just as in exercise 2, start counting. But only to ten this time. Then let your pelvis relax back into its normal state. Stay that way and relax for a count of ten, then repeat the entire exercise—twenty to thirty repeats in all.

A tip for advanced users: combining Kegels and reverse Kegels will give you what is known as anal breathing. This involves training the front and the back separately, performing the steps given for exercises 2 and 5 directly after each other. An exhibitionist bottom will enjoy using the rear version (anal breathing) as a visual stimulus. A twitching asshole will get every full-blooded stud feeling frisky.

▼ Exercise 7: Fire in Your Belly

Your abdominal muscles are sex muscles, purely on the basis of the aesthetic value they lend to parties and Pride parades. It is an unwritten law that the owner of a six-pack will always find someone to hook up with at any gay party. This may not only be due to the visual aspect but also to the sexual confidence radiated by anyone who owns a well-defined set of abs. Because there is another unwritten law that says if you've got a six-pack, you're good in bed—at least as a top.

This can be explained by the fact that in a good top, the propulsive force behind every thrust does not originate, as one might assume, in his legs, but rather in his core. It's easy to see why. Apart from

A six-pack looks hot and will help increase your sexual stamina as well.

the straight muscles you can see in a six-pack, there are also the oblique and traverse abdominals. The former are connected to the back, while the latter stretch down to the pelvic region. All of them work together to enable us to stand upright and to bend our torso to the side. The resulting key competence here is also the key to good sex: balance. Corresponding anatomically to the muscles along the spinal column, a well-defined set of abs will automatically guarantee better posture and more stability. These factors all result in an increase in the strength and purposefulness of what the Kama Sutra calls the "bull thrust." This should be enough in itself to demonstrate the benefits of working our your abs. So let's move on to the practical part, which in this case consists of five simple exercises you can integrate into your daily routine.

- **Jump rope:** you wouldn't think of it off-hand, but jumping rope is a great exercise for your abdominals—especially if you use a "speed step." This means that instead of jumping over the rope with your legs straight, you do it as if you were running—using alternate feet to jump off the ground. Jumping on one leg is another effective version. Do it the same number of times on each side. A quarter of an hour per day, three times a week is enough to kick-start your circulation, your metabolism, and your abs.

- **Medicine ball crunches:** absurdly enough, every personal trainer will advise against doing the infamous sit-ups if you're trying to build up a six-pack—as sit-ups are too specifically targeted and will strengthen the upper abs while neglecting all other areas. There is however a version of the "crunch," known as the sit-up's baby brother, which is still very popular. You lie on your back, your legs bent, and hold a ball between your thighs. A medicine ball is ideal, but a simple inflatable beach ball will do as well. Now hold your hands at the sides of your head and use your abs to slightly raise your upper body. Then raise your legs and move the ball in a circle with your knees. Put it down again after ten cycles and lower your upper body. Take a quick breather and then repeat the exercise ten times at least.

- **Stair climbing:** you can contract your muscles anywhere. So whenever you're just chilling out, watching TV or cooking, try sticking your gut out occasionally to check it's still there. You can also try drumming on it with your fists. A fun check-up method for part-time Neanderthals. But there's also a slightly more cultivated variation: stair climbing. Contracting your abs is especially effective here. And particularly if you take two steps at a time. It lends an entirely new meaning to the term "hot-stepper."

- **Pelvic lifts:** lie on your back, your arms flat on the ground next to your upper body and raise your legs so that they are at a right angle to your torso. Then lift up your ass without your arms leaving the gound. Hold for a few seconds until you feel a slight pull in your lower abs. Then lower your ass again. Repeat the exercise at least ten times.

- **Side bends:** this exercise targets the obliques. It's usually performed with dumbbells, but works just as well with any other weight you can hold easily, a water bottle for example. The rest is simple: stand with your legs apart, take the weight in your left hand and let it pull your upper body down to the side. Straighten up again, pulling the weight up with you. Repeat as much as you want. Then repeat the entire exercise on your right side.

▼ Exercise 8: Ass Sweepstakes

The tops all want to fuck it, the bottoms love to offer it up: a pert ass. In the last few years, this phenomenon within the gay community has lead to the proliferation of push-up briefs and debates about butt implants, which in my view are annoying simply because one glance is generally enough to realize how bogus these imitations really are. Plus they aren't necessary. Even without artificial aid, the gluteus maximus is a superlative in itself. Not only is it the largest muscle in the human body, it also one of the strongest (coming second after the mastication muscles). This should be reason enough to pay

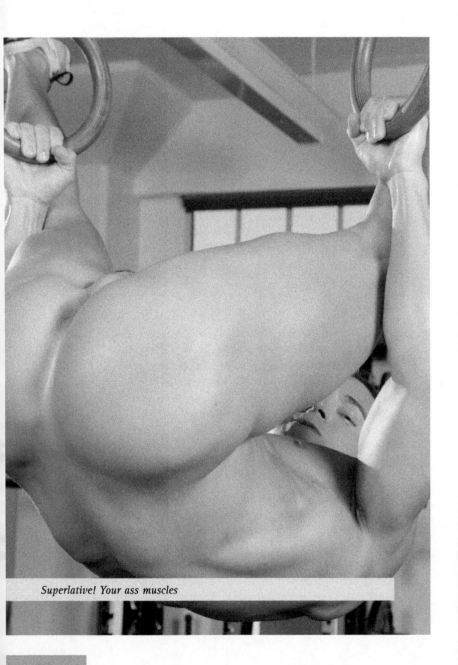

Superlative! Your ass muscles

as much attention to your own rear end as you pay to other guys' asses.

Now, after six training units I will understand if the *Gayma Sutra* class starts showing signs of tiring. Which is why I am pleased to announce: the last six lessons already comprise the main exercises for building up your ass muscles. Pelvic raises, stair climbing, squats, deadlifts and, last but not least, the big Kegel all play a part in strengthening your butt. So I will now declare the seventh sex gym round a sweepstake, where anyone can just pick his favorite exercise from the lessons on offer here. If you want to sit this one out, you also have my blessing to do so, but to get a feel for how easy it is to train your butt, I would like you to tense your ass muscles for five seconds ten times in a row while you're reading. You can do this while sitting, lying, standing, or squatting. So no copping out!

If you're up for a bonus round, I've got a fun but amazingly strenuous assignment for you—and it's also a good way to prepare for experimenting with different positions. Kneel on the ground, doggystyle, with your forearms on the ground. Then stretch your right leg back, holding it parallel to the gound. Briefly hold this position, then raise the outstretched leg until it's aligned with your upper body. Feel the tension in your ass muscles and count to ten. Then bring your leg back to its original position, parallel to the ground. Repeat as often as you like, and do the same number of repeats with your left leg. After all, you don't want to end up with one ass cheek more bubbly than the other. This drill is called "hip extensions" by the way. For a tempting bubble butt.

▼ Exercise 9: Tips for Your Nips

True love or tedium: on the question of nipples opinions differ widely. Some, equipped with well-developed nipples, swear by their erogenous powers, while others can't quite see what all the fuss is about. In my experience, their potential is directly attributable to differences in anatomy. By which I mean: the smaller and flatter your headlights are, the less of a pleasure factor. And a lower pleasure factor means a greater reluctance to let yourself in for tit play. But experience also shows that increasing the sensitivity of your raspberry ripples is simply a matter of practice. Initial reluctance can easily be supplanted by a fully fledged tit fetish with the proper treatment. And as arousal and erection of the nipples are in fact caused by muscle contractions, they cannot go unmentioned in this chapter. But before we go into the best tips for your nips, let's look at a couple of facts.

- **First:** male nipples are actually leftover from evolution. As their biological function (nursing babies), doesn't really apply to most guys, they have no real function.

- **Second:** nipples become hard and erect in response to cold, arousal or touch, due to a reaction of the smooth muscle tissue that forms part of their anatomy. This reaction is a reflex similar to the one that causes goose bumps. It can be deliberately induced, but not controlled in the strict sense of the word (unlike contracting your biceps, for instance).

- **Third:** Nipple size is genetically determined. But being made of very soft tissue, they can be stretched quite far. Heavy strain can even cause permanent stretching. If you've ever made even the smallest incursion into the gay fetish scene, you'll have met characters with extremely large, elongated nipples—the result of years of stretching. Apart from the tit torture classic with your fingers, this may involve nipple suction cups, clamps, pumps, and piercing. Moving on, it's time to tackle our selection of tit-bits, which is more of a journey of discovery in four levels that a proper workout.

- **Level 1:** Stand in front of a mirror and take a good look at your nipples. Particularly hairy guys may want to shave their chests first. Your nipples themselves don't grow hair, but they do tend to disappear under a thick pelt. As constantly pushing aside swathes

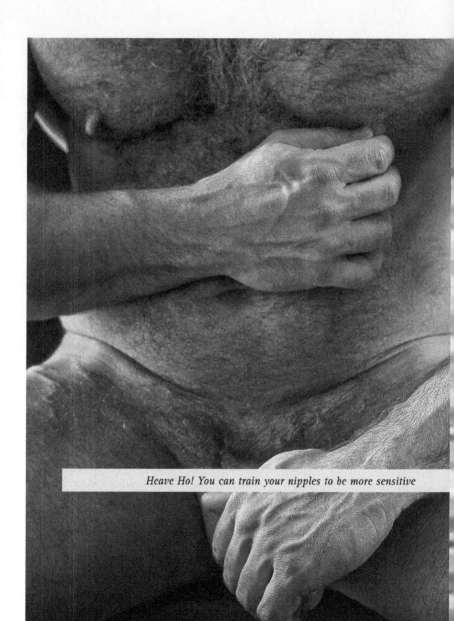

Heave Ho! You can train your nipples to be more sensitive

65

of hair won't make your discovery journey any easier, it makes sense to shave off a few square inches. Don't worry, it'll grow back. Then wet your nipples with cold water or saliva and blow on them. This should result in a palpable nipple erection, which you can encourage by flicking them with your thumb, as if you were plucking a guitar string.

- **Level 2:** Heave ho! Pinch your nipple between your thumb and forefinger and carefully pull it away from your body until it starts to hurt. The unpleasant sensation will make most people quit at this point. Understandable enough, but if you really want to get a kick out of it, you should try to analyze the sensations created by squeezing and pulling. This means: let go, feel the pain subside, and see how blowing and flicking them as described in level 1 feels. Your nipple will react to being squeezed by getting even harder, which can be arousing. If that is the case, you will automatically squeeze and pull at it again, and now you're well on your way to being seduced by the attractions of nipple play. So if your early explorations wind up turning into a protracted session, don't be alarmed if your nipples feel kind of rough and chapped for a few days afterwards. The skin on your nipples is very sensitive and unaccustomed friction can lead to chafing. No big deal. A dollop of skin cream will fix that.

- **Level 3:** Let's play! Get to know your limits by telling your lover to suck or carefully nibble at your nipples. Make sure you don't have a clumsy hothead spoiling your fun by biting down too hard. To increase your nipples' sensitivity, you can also use the pumps and suction cups mentioned above. To use these flexible plastic cups, moisten the edges, squeeze them together and apply them your nipples, where they will stay due to the vacuum you've created. In theory, you can apply the same principle to empty plastic bottles. But only in theory. The size of the bottles and the openings prevents them from having quite the desired effect, this being to make your nipples larger and more sensitive, so that you can have more fun with them once you've taken the cups off.

- **Level 4:** Test your pain threshold. If you can tolerate a clothes peg, you're doing pretty well, if you have pierced nipples, you're a pro, and if you're using alligator clamps, you're definitely one of the toughest cookies out there. But don't overdo it, big guy. You don't want to wear them out.

▼ Exercise 10: The King of Variety

No sex gym would be complete without the classic push-up. There's no need for me to explain how to do this simple body weight exercise, but perhaps I should explain what it's got to do with your sex life.

- **Point 1:** First of all, there's the instant visual effect. If you do a couple of quick sets of push-ups just before a date or a party, not only will your tits and biceps feel bigger, they actually will -be

Eyes down and keep pumping!
Push-ups are the single most effective bodyweight exercise

bigger. Provided you're pretty fit as it is, of course, otherwise you won't be able to do "a quick set" anyway. But that's precisely what we're here for now.

- **Point 2:** Apart from your chest, your shoulders, and your back, push-ups primarily target your arms. And these play an extremely important part in most sex positions. Whether you're holding, supporting, lifting, or gripping yourself or your partner, your arms are always in action. Many positions would simply be impossible to do without your arms. Additionally, I can think of least three positions, the "big dipper," the "fitness missionary," and the "double-decker" offhand, that are directly based on or utilize the push-up motion. Any questions?

- **Point 3:** Their are over fifty variations on the push-up. This makes it a great way to demonstrate how one basic exercise can have many variations, and this can be directly applied to exploring sex positions. The common or garden push-up involves raising and lowering your extended body with your arms. But you can also do this with one arm, one leg, with or without clapping, on your knees or your toes, with lunges, hops, with your arms bent or stretched, on your fists, your fingertips, and so on and so forth.

This should be enough for you to get started, and you are definitely permitted to add your own interpretations. That way, you'll never get bored with your workout. To keep this up, I recommend having clear and realistic expectations. Beginners can start out with doing thirty push-ups every two days. It doesn't matter when, where, or how you do them. Do one set of ten every morning, afternoon, and evening, or do thirty in one go. Do them in the park, at home, in your bathroom. It's all up to you, but make sure you've reached thirty by the time you go to bed. Once you start feeling an improvement, raise the number of repeats. If you want to outsmart yourself, you can do double units and count two push-ups as one. This ruse actually works for me. I feel less exhausted if I count to ten instead of twenty—even though I know that I have to kiss the ground twice for every number. One more thing: before you start pumping, always take a moment to circle your shoulders and your wrists and stretch your arms to warm your body up.

▼ Exercise 11: The Anal Oracle

This takes us to the holy of holies: your anus. Made up of two sphincters as well as all kinds of glands and nerve cells, it is seen as the embodiment of gay sexuality. Which is a misconstruction in my opinion, because in my own experience, the embodiment of gay sexuality is the dick. How else do you explain the relatively high number of homos you meet who don't know how to treat their own assholes, or even refer to themselves as "exclusive tops" and declare their holes a no-go area? The former condition is treatable, the latter indicates a lack of willingness to experiment, which I can only attribute to laziness. Any man who takes the time and effort necessary to explore and become acquainted with his own asshole and the delicacies that lie beyond it should be a stranger to the dangers of exclusivity. This is my message to all of you who until now have taken the view that your own asshole is too good, too dirty, too inexperienced, or too tight to poke around in. I'm putting this very bluntly, as I have raised all these objections myself, and interpret them, in retrospect, merely as an expression of different stages of underdevelopment. So let's take care of them quickly and painlessly.

Too good: Arrogance never got anyone a really good fuck. So if parts of your body are too good for you to include in the full-body pastime of sexual endeavor, you're only depriving yourself.

Too dirty: Right, the whole shit thing, which even the most diligent douche experts never seem to be able to come to grips with ... The problem can only really be dealt with by routine and realism. Nobody will ever be able to change the irreuftable fact that the anus is the site of the final stages of digestion. On the other hand, your body's self-cleaning processes are pretty functional, so the whole shit, shower, and shag routine generally works quite well. Accidents can always happen. As long as they aren't caused by gross negligence, this is pardonable. But if you realize you've got a log lodged halfway, do the decent thing and spend the evening as an "exclusive top" for a change.

Too inexperienced: We'll make this one snappy! We've all been inexperienced, but there's never any call to stay that way. So get off your ass and learn something new!

Too tight: How shall I put it? Yes, we've all been tight as well. And yes, there's no call to stay that way, either. So open your ass and learn something new!

Now that that's dealt with, let's forge ahead and learn something new. As in the "tips for your nips," we can take a four level approach to accomplishing this. And let's not forget, we're not in sex-ed class here, we're at the sex gym. After all, we have to start out by taming our sphincter muscles before gaining access to the anal oracle.

- **Level 1:** Shower, dry yourself off, haul a mattress in front of the largest mirror in your house, and keep a bottle of lube or Vaseline to hand. Lie on your back on the mattress, bend your legs, and scoot your butt as close to the mirror as possible. Pull your ass cheeks apart with both hands, push your sphincter outwards (see exercise 5), and probe it with your fingers. Look in the mirror to observe how your anus reacts.

- **Level 2:** Using a circling movement, massage a dollop of lube into your anus. Relax. Then push your sphincter out again and

Where's the entrance? Evan Matthews exploring his "ring of fire"

carefully push your index finger into your hole. Your sphincter will generally react to being penetrated by contracting. Don't be alarmed and make the mistake of withdrawing your finger. It needs to stay in the hole until the muscle relaxes again, allowing you to slowly, and then more quickly, push your finger back and forth. Your goal is now to gradually insert it deeper and deeper, without rushing things. Take your time to explore your anal cavity, feel for your prostate and try and enjoy the sensations it arouses. If you find your dick getting hard, you're doing it right, but even if you don't, it will probably react by secreting a few drops of pre-cum.

- **Level 3:** The goal is expansion. To familiarize yourself with pushing through your sphincter and to gradually get it accustomed to the bigger guns, I recommend you start using more fingers, and then other aids. If you don't have a dildo, you really can use carrots (for beginners) and cucumbers (advanced level)—even though it is a bit of a cliché. When buying your veggies, make sure they have a smooth surface and a rounded tip. For reasons of hygiene, please slip a condom over them before using. And anything you insert into your body should also be at body temperature. Do not use anything straight from the refrigerator! Your sphincter is very sensitive to cold. I only mention all of this in passing. Basically, I would strongly advise against using improvised toys. They will only mess up your first steps for you. In my earlier days, lacking funds, I have abused the occasional cucumber myself, as well as bottle necks, deodorant cans, and screwdriver handles. And when I finally did purchase an anal toy, it was the cheapest one on offer: a weird lady's dildo with a ribbed shaft. Bullshit! It's better to invest just a bit more cash in a proper penis replica to really get an idea of what it's like to have a dick in your ass for the first time. You'll never be entirely prepared for the first time your ass is broached, but using a dildo is definitely a lot better than fucking your dinner. You'll hopefully graduate from jelly rubber to real flesh soon enough.

- Level 4: Congratulations! You've left your "exclusive" phase behind you, now it's time to determine whether you're on your way to becoming a pro-level bottom or doomed to remain an average fuckee. I've called this stage the butt plug level. Acquiring one of these oval broad-based plug dildos will mark the transition of your butt fuck from the intimacy of your bedroom to daily life. If you aspire to become a real power bottom, insert the thing into your ass first thing in the morning, go grocery shopping or to work or university, and don't take it out until your next hookup. This is a great way of placing bets on your own endurance. It took me quite a number of tries before I managed to keep my plug in for an entire day. So if it starts to feel uncomfortable, pop it out and try again next day. If you keep at it, your anal oracle may one day whisper the words you crave: "exclusive bottom" in your ear.

Part 2

Foot Frotting, Belly Rubbing, and the Somersault Shot: Masturbation Positions

Masturbation is held in low esteem by many. Their loss, is all I can say. I would claim that every man has had more sex with himself in the course of his life than with anyone else. So it would be a colossal waste of time to discount this kind of sex as merely a means to an end. But above all, it's a crime against yourself. Jacking off aimlessly, just to get some relief from your own horniness, often results in a lingering sense of guilt for most people. Nagging scruples left over from puberty are coupled with macho views of the solitary orgasm as a waste of energy. You can combat both of these by adding more variety and commitment to your solo efforts and turning them into a more satisfying experience—which is what they should be. This will also inevitably involve experimenting with different positions. Time for the wanker's workshop!

▼ Lying Down

▷ On Your Back—Top Ten

Before you all collectively yawn at me: I do realize that lying on your back and rubbing one out isn't a position, it's an institution—but it still has its place here. For one thing, I think it's both sensible and convenient to pique your interest in the big beat-off by starting out at a point of consensus and letting your appetite gradually grow from them there. For another, because experiementing with sexual positions is a bit like sports: it's best to warm up first before you embark on the complicated moves. And finally, beating off in a supine position is similar to push-ups in our sex gym: there are endless variations. So here are the top ten variations on a classic move—again, listed in increasing order. So let's view the whole thing as an awakening, a new beginning.

- **Ten: With your eyes closed**
  Are you sleeping, or are you wanking, Brother John? There are no official surveys on what a guy looks at while jerking off. But as the numbers of men who use porn are at around eighty to ninety percent in western countries, depending on which survey you read, we can safely assume that as a rule, visual cues are common—which we will simply dispense with for our *Gayma Sutra* awakening. The stimulus is as simple as the position. Lie down flat, no pillows behind your neck, under your butt or knees, on the rug or a mattress, and let your own personal mind movie put you in the mood. The fantasies that play out before your inward eye can often tell you a lot about your hidden sexual desires. Enjoy your solo performance!

- **Nine: With your eyes on the ceiling**
  Slightly more difficult! Open your eyes and stare at the ceiling, without looking at your crotch. Your imagination will be at work here, too, but this time it will be distracted by the bare reality posed by the ceiling, without being offered any sort of visual erotic stimulus (mirrored ceilings don't count). This forces you to shift your focus from imaginary images to your body's reactions. Purist masturbation can revolutionize your body awareness.

- **Eight: Use the "other hand"**
  Your average Joe Jack-off will generally use his "main fist"—right-handers use the right hand and lefties use the left. Switching hands not only challenges your motor skills, it can also result in the interesting sensation of rediscovering yourself. Two more advantages are: it trains the less-used part of your brain, and your boner will feel larger to your "inexperienced" hand for some reason.

Lying on your back, eyes on your crotch. There's no shame in ogling yourself while you're rubbing one out.

- **Seven: Twist your fist**
  You can achieve a similar effect to that of the "other hand" by turning your hand around. Just stretch out your arm and turn your hand around 180 degrees so that the ring formed by your forefinger and thumb points downwards. The unfamiliar reversal of the way the pressure is distributed over your fingers, your palm, and the heel of your hand is an eye-opener!

- **Six: With your legs crossed**
  We're still masturbating while lying flat on our backs, but this time we're going to cross our legs. This acts as a kind of emergency brake. Squeezing your balls and your pelvic floor increases the tension. You can vary this effect by switching legs from time to time. Uncross your legs just before you cum.

- **Five: With your eyes on your crotch**
  Besides the purist version and the movie playing in your head, we mustn't forget the narcissist's version of masturbation. It makes sense if you're gay. Whatever the self-appointed ethics commission may tell you, there's no shame in ogling yourself while you're rubbing one out . If you're into dicks, then be happy you've got one yourself, and one hard-on in the room is better than none at all. Anyway, you have to love your own penis to give generously to others. So, stick a cushion behind your neck and crank up the ego-porn.

- **Four: With both hands**
  If you're not already a habitual lube user while masturbating, now is the time to start. Rubbing your own cock between your palms (or the backs of your hands) in a dry state will let you in for a bumpy ride, but once you're lubed up, it will be a match for any fleshjack or silicon pussy.

- **Three: With your legs spread**
  While crossing your legs acts as an emergency brake, spreading them will open the floodgates. Despite its predictability, this

wanking position is the most liberating of them all. Its literally "open" stance will give your subconscious the green light to let itself go. That's why you so often assume this position when climaxing. Consciously masturbating in this position from the start will accelerate your pleasure. Gentlemen with especially thick and heavy balls will be even more aware of the package resting between their legs.

- Two: With a cushion under your butt
Take it out from behind your neck and stick it under your ass! A cushion under your butt will turn your supine wank into a volcano of lust. By raising your trunk and thereby arching your body back, your butt muscles will automatically tighten the more aroused you get, so that the energy rushing into your loins will also appear to be pushed upwards into your boner. Your ensuing eruption will be twice as hot.

- One: Cumming without touching
As Oscar Wilde once said: "To do nothing at all is the most difficult thing in the world, the most difficult and the most intellectual." It is doubtful that this man of letters was referring to solitary sex at the time, but it's still very apt. The ability to reach orgasm without touching your dick is one of the highest achievements of erotic self-channeling, and in this age of sensory overload, it is an almost completely forgotten skill. I don't mean that you should make this a daily practice, but as a ritual experiment it has its own attraction. And after four days of ejaculatory abstinence (or more or less, depending on your individual libido), it can be a truly gripping experience! Really strict adherents of the no-touch method insist on total reduction—just pelvic floor pumping and mental ecstasy, with no additional stimulus. This is ambitious, but a bit too much. For beginners in particular, not touching their dicks will be challenge enough. I think we can agree that factoring in other stimuli (from sex chats to porn or anal massage) is complete legitimate.

▶ Intercrural Sex (Solo)

It is time to leave the extended position behind us. For solitary intercrural sex, pull up both your legs to your trunk in a fetal position and wrap your thighs around your hard-on. But first grease it up with lots of lube so that it can smoothly slip and slide between your thighs, which you are now rubbing together, gradually getting faster. A lot of people take some time to get used to the unfamiliar horizontal stimulation, but once you've jizzed between your own thighs, you'll drop all your reservations. Verticality fetishists can move their pelvis to jerk their dicks back and forth if they like, but in this position, this is more likely to wear you out than to turn you on.

▶ The Double Ring

For this position, stay lying on your back, pull your legs up, and open them. Stabilize your position by hooking your lower arms under your knees. Then make two rings with the forefinger and thumb of each hand. One ring goes around your scrotum, just above your balls, the other goes around your boner. Now start whacking off. As both your hands will be reaching through your thighs from below, it won't be easy at first to hit your rhythm. But once you get going, the ring stimulation on your dick and the added bonus of being able to stretch your balls is what makes this method so hot.

▶ The Somersault Shot

It's time to get moving. The somersault shot is a really fun move to do, not least because it offers you the opportunity to shoot your load in your own face when you cum. It's convoluted, but not impossible. Lie down on your back and raise your legs up into the candle pose, which you probably know from yoga or gymnastics class. Then open your legs up to form a diamond shape over your head, with your feet, soles together, forming the tip. The rest is a matter of balance. Try and let the diamond formed by your legs

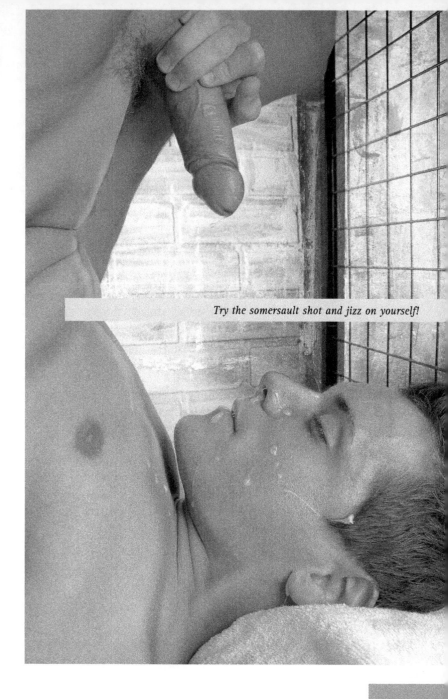

fall backwards so that your dick points straight at your face. Then use one hand to jerk off with, while stabilizing your hip with the other. This should culminate in a facial shower, which the really athletic may want to top with a backward roll. Everyone else, myself included, can just roll forwards.

▷ The Mattress Thrust

The method of pushing two beds or mattresses together, in order to rub your hard shaft back and forth in the crack, has a long history. In the 19th century, apparently, the Brits called this the "Chinese position" as it was popular among patrons of shady nightclubs, who performed this move while high on opium, with the obligatory post-ejaculatory comment: "Now we've given a little life to China." This refers to the load of semen shot towards the gound which, if a tunnel were to be drilled straight through the globe, would have landed on the other side of the world, in China. A more convincing explanation would be the Chinese prostitutes who would crouch under the beds, but we'll be coming back to that in our oral sex chapter. For now, all I can say is that, personally, the mattress thrust doesn't do it for me. It's always a stop-gap solution, it's always uncomfortable, and it always carries a high risk of injury for your penis. But if you want to try it out anyway, for the sake of completeness, then please put a condom on first and make sure that the mattresses are covered with fitted sheets made of smooth fabric. A light version of this practice is to lie on your front and rub yourself on the mattress. Instead of frotting your hard-on between two external surfaces, you rub it between the padding underneath you and your belly.

▼ Sitting Down

▷ The Basic Sit-in

I'm going to just subsume anything that's not lying down or standing up under the category sitting. This also includes kneeling and squatting down. But I'll be starting out with the classic chair position. I call this one the "Basic Sit-in" because it reminds me of the poster for *Basic Instinct 2*, the one with Sharon Stone straddling a chair and leering at the camera. That's just to explain the name. The rest is definitely loads better than the Sharon Stone's wannabe lascivious look and the completely pointless film. The first point is not to use an office chair with a closed back, but rather a simple kitchen chair with a window between the seat and the back. That way, you can sit astride it while sticking your boner through the opening. And then it's showtime. When you bend forwards, the back of the chair supports your chest, leaving both hands free to take care of your hard-on. At the same time, you can watch what you're doing from above. On the one hand, this is very comfortable, on the other, the chair frame clenched between your legs will create an enjoyable pressure on your inner thighs, which you can increase or decrease at will. No wonder this sit-in generally finishes with a bang.

▶ **The Heel-Splayer**

This is a position to literally get down on your knees for. The heel-splayer is more than just a dick-frotting position, it's a gift to your asshole. First you kneel upright. Your insteps should be laid flat on the floor, your heels should be touching. Then pull your ass-cheeks apart with your hands and squat right down. Your open crack should come directly into contact with your feet, so that your heels are pushed between your butt cheeks. That way they keep your cheeks spread apart once you've taken your hands away. By carefully splaying your heels, you can spread your crack even wider.

Now if you reach between your legs from the front and move your fingers up your taint, they'll hit a wide open ass funnel, just waiting for your hand or toys to move in. While you're doing that. your free hand can take care of your front.

▶ Lotus Love

The lotus position is one of the basic yoga poses, where your legs are placed over each other, similar to sitting cross-legged, but with both feet resting on the opposite thighs. This creates a stable sitting pose for meditating and guarantees that energy can flow through your body unimpeded. We're not here to meditate, but the energy flow isn't such a bad place to start. So—stretch your limbs, tie your legs in knots, and wank away? Well ... as I don't wish to be held responsible for strains and cramps among my readers, I do need to warn you that "sitting" comfortably in the lotus pose will take a certain amount of flexibility, and it took me a couple of weeks to master. It then took me couple more days to keep up an erection for any amount of time while tying myself in knots. By now, I have really come to appreciate the stability and devotion of this pose. And spreading your semen over your crossed legs after you've completed your mission can make the somewhat esoteric idea of energy flow sexily palpable. For the sake of completeness I'll also add that real yoga freaks can also do the "reverse lotus"—the same thing, only standing on your head. If you can do the reverse lotus love, you deserve a medal.

▶ Foot-Frotting

This brings us to a method way over my personal pay grade, but out of deference to its attraction and to honor the foot fetish-ists among us, I shall be mentioning it anyway. Foot-frotters are people who definitely do not have any difficulties doing the lotus pose. On top of that, they are in possession of the enviable quality of being able to masturbate with their own feet. To do this, they sit down with their backs against the wall and spread their legs into the diamond we mentioned earlier in a different context, with the soles of their feet meeting at the tip. So far, so simple. But now, turning your feet ninety degrees upward and pushing your erect penis through the narrow opening between your soles ... well, you try it. It is feasible, as I witnessed firsthand with my ex-boyfriend, but this guy is a professional dancer and accordingly very flexible.

So please don't feel inadequate if foot frotting turns out to be too much for you.

For you hardcore fans of autoerotic experimentation with your feet, I also recommend another variation involving only one foot. Just pull one of your feet up to your crotch and, depending on how flexible you are, use either your heel or your sole to rub your boner against your belly.

Please don't forget to use lube. While the relatively rough skin on your feet does make up part of this type of stimulation's attraction, not using any goo at all will make it pretty uncomfortable.

▶ Autofellatio

I've already mentioned this in our chapter on what the pros are doing, but I've not yet gone into details of how to do it. Autofellatio is sucking yourself off. If you can do it, kudos to you. Everyone else may take comfort in the fact that ninety-seven percent of the male popula-

Additional information: Ricky Martinez is 12 x 9 inches.

tion can't do it either. But we're not here to prematurely throw in the towel. Everyone should try tonguing their own glans at least once. Even if it's just to gain a greater appreciation of your lover's fellating skills. One possible method would incorporate the somersault shot, then propping your butt up against a wall or the couch and pushing yourself down with both hands. But that would be making things unnecessarily difficult for yourself. For a more promising method, we return to the kitchen chair employed in the basic sit-in. This time, you sit on it the right way and grip the seat with your stronger hand while grasping the root of your dick with the other. Are you sitting securely? And has your cock reached its highest level of stiffness? Then proceed. Lower your chin towards your chest, hunch your back and, using your hand on the seat, pull yourself down towards your boner as hard as you can. You can use the hand on your dick to assist by pushing your member upwards. Have I already mentioned training your tongue every morning for the benefit of your rimming skills? This is where this training will unexpectedly pay off. All I can say is: try licking pre-cum from your own glans for once in your life—but it's not a life-changing experience.

And after hunching our backs for so long, it's time to straighten up again. So let's move on to the standing positions.

▼ Standing Up

▶ Fucking a Melon

The thing with the carrots and the cucumbers was to keep your ass happy. Now let's find a healthy option for your dick. Cutting a hole in a melon, digging yourself a fuck-channel and then—I beseech you!—first putting a condom on your dick and sticking it in is above all an unholy mess. Another complication is added by the fact that it is extremely difficult to get the stubborn piece of fruit to assume the right temperature, neither too cold (normal temperature) nor too hot (after briefly heating it in the oven, always check with your finger to make sure no heat pockets have formed inside). The sole positive aspect to this exercise is also the reason why it's even worth mentioning in the context of sexual positions. Let's be honest here: standing in the middle of the room holding the fat round fruit in front of your crotch, thrusting hard with your hips, and driving your wang into it and feeling the sticky pulp running down your thighs with every thrust ... that's pretty hot. The sheer mass of your fuck-fruit is the main cause for this. Its weight will absorb your thrusts while keeping you grounded. In this way, it compensates for any balance issues that are a common by-product of masturbating on your feet. In brief: it's an interesting alternative to most other masturbators, which generally aim for lightness and ergonomic design. But fucking a melon still isn't an everyday activity.

▷ The Doppelganger

I have already alluded to the narcissist aspect of gay masturbation. For a (literally) upright celebration of this quality, we'll go on a wank date with our own reflection. Ideally, you should have a full-length mirror in your apartment for this, but taking down a more standard sized one from your bathroom wall works as well.

This isn't so much about caressing your own image as it is about observing parts of your body from an unfamiliar perspective. The sensation of the mirror's smooth, cool surface on your skin lends an extra thrill. But to unleash the "Doppelganger's" true pornographic potential, get your lubed-up wang right up against the mirror when you cum. Hot stuff! But don't forget to clean it off before the next family visit!

▶ The Divinely Hot Tripod

The *Kama Sutra* is based on the Hindu faith. The Hindu gods may have ten arms (Durga), four faces (Brahma), or even an elephant's trunk (Ganesh). So why shouldn't a *Gayma Sutra* masturbator, inspired by the combined strength of the lotus, the somersault, and the melon, have three legs? Habitual bottoms have a clear advantage with this divinely hot beat-off method. The tripod earns his extra limb by sticking it in his butt. The idea is to place a dildo upright on the ground, to stand over it, and without using your hands, insert it into your anus by slowly squatting down on it. You should pre-

pare both your sphincter and the dildo with a generous coating of lube first, and be either an excellent deadlifter or a well-versed bottom. Generally, the sex toy industry follows the rule of "the greater the breadth of a dildo, the greater the length." So if you choose an especially thick artificial wang as your third leg, you won't have to squat down so far.

The real challenge, however, isn't so much inserting the thing, but rather the part that comes next. That's when you learn to walk with your third leg. To prevent your sexy extra limb from sliding out right away, it's best to use one with a thick ridge below the tip.

▶ The Belly Rub

The belly rub completely dispenses with toys or sensual extrava-ganzas. It's a kind of organic variation on the Doppelganger. This means you also press your lubed-up dick up against your belly and rub it until you climax. But this time you don't use a mirror, just the palms of your hands. Of course, you can do this lying down as well, but standing up has the advantage of being able to control the pressure with your loins instead of a flat surface. This will give you "Good Vibrations." In any case: for optimum enjoyment, don't be too sparing with the lube. Tugging at your balls also works as a very nice addition to this vertical practice.

▶ The Crab Wanker

The crab walk has gained a kind of icky fame via *The Exorcist*, so I'm going to reclaim it for onanistic purposes. Not without an ulterior motive, of course. The crab wanker is a first-class way to prepare yourself for the "Great Crab Thrust" in our chapter on oral sex, as well as the "Double-Decker" in the anal sex chapter and the bull ride in the group sex chapter. This position is also to insulate me against any accusations of letting the ego-hedonism of these masturbation lessons lose sight of their use value for future challenges. And so here's the incredibly simple implementation: start out with you and (your dick) standing up, lower yourself back into the crab position, take a couple of crab steps, and then raise a hand to take care of your dick. The great thing about this is the way it combines different techniques. If your supporting arm starts to tire, just switch hands. And if your jerking-off begins to tire, try thrusting your hips. And if your self-control starts to flag, then blow your wad. See you at the crab thrust.

▶ At an Angle

If I wanted, I could start the new category "in mid-air" for methods like this one. But I don't want to. After all, you can easily move into this two-step ritual from an upright position, and so it works beautifully as a transition from solitary gratification to sex with a partner. And this is how you do it: hold a thick cushion against the wall at the level of your hips and lean your head against it so that your body is at a right angle to the wall and the floor. With your head up against the wall, you'll have both hands free for whacking off. And gazing into the frame made up out of the wall, the ground and your body gives you a pleasant sensation of closed-off intimacy. You can enhance this sensation by moving down a story and stuffing the cushion into the corner between the wall and the floor. Laying your head on this will turn it into the front end of a bridge, with your feet at the other end and your boner pointing towards the ground at its highest point. So much for only teenagers spitting off of bridges and only hobos watching from underneath them. Right angle wankers are proof to the contrary—they like to do both. At the same time.

And now that's enough of solitary sex. It's time for a partner.

Interlude: One for the Money, Two for the Show

When you've spent any amount of time on your own, you need to get used to having a second man there with you. This applies not only to your love life but to any book on the subject as well. So after this extensive introduction, training, and beating off, we won't jump straight back into fucking, but rather approach our new partners with what some young adult publications might call "petting." You might think this is the soft approach—but truth be told, erotic exchanges that go beyond obvious oral and anal moves can lay bare the hard core of what attracts you physically. Turning off the full-speed-ahead-to-orgasm mode will give you the opportunity to explore your partner's anatomy, his smell, and his preferences.

The fact is, you generally don't realize this until the first sexual rush has subsided. But if you never get beyond this rush in any relationship, then the soft approach to the hard core is probably the best for you. After all, there are different positions you can try out here, too. Here's an interlude for getting to know each other.

▷ Kiss Climbing

Not even the most exotic move can turn you on the same way as a really intense kiss. Although ... in a way, a really intense kiss is a position in itself. While you're nibbling on your latest make-out partner, you tend to intuitively start "climbing." Your partner becomes a Mount Everest of desire and your lips are the crampons of lust. Passionate embraces, entwining your legs, grasping with your hands ... all moves are allowed when you're kiss climbing. This can be performed while still clothed, up against walls, fences, and cars after hooking up at a bar or a club. Many a guy has cum while doing this, without even unzipping his pants. So you can just imagine the potential for this position once you lose the clothes.

▷ The Lie-Down Test

The name sounds kind of workman-like, but it's actually the exact opposite. For this position, both partners lie in each other's arms, gazing into one another's eyes. It doesn't matter whether you're making out, licking, or just looking at each other. The main thing is that this is the perfect position for reaching the right temperature. You can feel the warmth of your partner's body and the guy on top can increase the pressure gently or more intensely by letting his entire weight sink into his lover's body. This can be especially sexy if both participants keep their underpants on at first and rub their stiffening dicks together through the thin fabric. That's why this particular discipline is often called frottage (from the French "frotter"–"to rub"). Have the guy underneath bend his knees and lift the other guy up with his pelvis for an erotic mid-air experience.

▶ The Foot in the Door

If your daily routine is interrupted by lust, many of you won't even make it to the bedroom. Which means: the action starts getting hot and heavy on counter tops, bars, or the kitchen table. But is it truly real desire? There's one safe method of measuring your partner's arousal, and that's shoving your thigh between his legs. For example: while lying on your back and letting him pamper you, casually push your knee between your benefactor's legs. If you lets you do it, you've got a foot in the door. By raising your leg or clenching your thigh muscles, you can massage his dick and his balls, while continuing to enjoy his caresses. This trick has another bonus: if one of your legs is between his, then inevitably one of his legs will be between your own. It's a win-win situation.

▶ Intercrural Fucking

This isn't quite fucking, but close enough. Intercrural intercourse has a long history, famous for the role it played in ancient Greece, where teachers would practice this method with their students. In the meantime, it has gone rather out of fashion, but simulating anal sex has not lost any of its attraction. The basic idea is to insert your erect penis between your partner's legs. There are many variations on this theme. These are the top three.

- **Jacked up:** The bottom lies on his back with his legs raised, while the top kneels behind him and sticks his boner in between his thighs. This gives you the opportunity to try out different rhythms and speeds, without the finality of anal penetration. The guy kneeling down would be well-advised to grease up his dick with

lube or saliva first. The rest is pure sensation. As the friction is focused directly at the point where the thighs meet your ass crack, the "jacked up" method is a first class technique for creating good vibrations—and for the top, it's also a great way of building up your ass and calves.

- **Reversed:** As before, the recipient lies on his back with his legs bent. But this time, the top kneels over him instead of behind. He does this by turning his back on the bottom and sitting across his loins. That way, both participants can concentrate on their own sensations without being distracted by their partner's gaze. But a quick glance over your shoulder is always worth your while. Even if it's just to catch a glimpse of the bottom lying there with his eyes closed, licking his lips voluptuously. In any case, you should always have some lube at hand here as well. Depending on how slippery you are, you can try out different power modes in this position. Supporting himself with his hands on the bed and holding a push-up position, the top can ram his boner into the gap between the other guy's thighs from above. Or the guy on the bottom can bend his legs more and push his lover's cock back and forth between his thighs. But simply the sight of your lover's back will probably be enough for most people.

- **Curled up:** The bottom lies on his back curled up in the fetal position, with his arms clasped behind his knees. He can them raise his lower legs to signal "Action!" Clasping his arms behind his knees makes his position stable enough for the top to come up from behind and roll him back and forth until he finds the ideal point and the ideal angle for insertion. This position also squeezes the bottom's legs together, tightening up the gap between his thighs.

▷ **Behind the Knees**

The name says it all really. The backs of the knees are to this position what the thigh gap is to the intercrural method. The best way to do this is to have the bottom lie on his back with his knees bent,

while the top inserts his member into the gap from the side. The natural curve of the calf muscles will encircle your dick especially tightly and increase stimulation. But this also means a greater risk of injury. So if you're going to plunge right in, it's best to use lube and a condom. For a more comfortable variation on the procedure, the guy lying down stretches his leg out over his partner's wang and lets him close down the shutter on his member.

▶ A Finger in the Pie

Time to loosen up your fingers! Or to be precise, use your fingers to loosen up his sphincter. Purists will proceed systematically here. The recipient offers up his hole by sticking out his rear end while supporting his upper body against a table or the side of the bed. Mr. Finger should kneel down behind him and get to work. This is not the most comfortable method of engaging with someone's sphincter, but its advantage lies in its concentration on the essentials. This position offers anal newcomers in particular the space they need to concentrate. With your arms or hands supported by a solid surface, you can feel your hole being massaged without being distracted by the ceiling or by sinking mattresses. Nor do you have to spend energy on spreading your legs.

At the same time, the finger fucker can observe how his partner's body reacts—while also rubbing his dick up and down his calf.

Crossing the Border to Melon Head: Positions for Oral Sex

We've already had a lesson on the theory of deep throating in the sex gym chapter—now it's time for the practical part. As a matter of fact, blow jobs often set the stage for how your sexual encounter will progress. If you botch this one, you risk screwing up all the closeness you've built up, which generally has a negative effect on any future hookups. So what do we conclude from this? It's best to have a realistic appraisal of your own blow job skills, and when you're doing the deed, stay within your own personal skill set.

Deliberately taking certain positions can help with this. For a dick with an exaggerated upwards curve, a head down position such as the 69 is best. For the especially large calibers, try a control position like the "Oral Office" and the strong thrust of the "Melon Head" position can make a small boner feel larger. If you like, you can adjust the model for dick size and hole-depth compatibility from our "Pole Position" chapter to oral sex. Just substitute mouths for assholes in the category hole depth. For the sake of clarity, I have divided up the following positions into the categories "Get Your Dick Out!" and "Open Up!" The first category focuses on positions in which the blow job giver determines the rhythm, the second on the ones where the rhythm is controlled by the recipient. "Eat Ass!" is a category of its own. And now we've had enough chitchat. Get your dick out, open up and eat ass!

▼ Get Your Dick Out!

▷ The Top Ten 69ers

Starting off our blow-by-blow account with the indisputable classic, the 69, is simply a matter of respect. This position is the pinnacle of oral sex, being one of the very few sexual positions where both participants can do the same thing—in this case, suck dick. On the one hand, this means both partners are equally top and bottom, but as most guys' multitasking skills will be completely exhausted by simultaneously swallowing and being swallowed, thrusting does not play much of a role in this context. So we're in the right place in the "Get Your Dick Out!" section. The rest is simply a question of how creative you are. A position whose name depicts the mirrored but identical position of its participants using a number with mirrored but identical digits should be carried out with the same degree of imaginativeness. There's definitely room for more than simply following the classic one-up-one-down principle. Here's a list of the top ten variations.

- Ten: A First Taste
  We'll start off with an exquisite tip and foreskin hors d'ouevre. Both of you crouch down in the 69 position, but increase your anticipation by refusing to perform an actual blow job. Instead, exclusively concentrate on the tip, pampering it with your lips and tongue. Carefully sucking at the foreskin or the piss-slit not only gives you a first taste of your lover's aroma, but also of the ultimate joys of the 69er. The longer you manage to keep up the tasting phase, the greater your satisfaction will be when you finally take the plunge.

- Nine: The Vampire
  If you happen to have a monkey bar or a loft bunk at home, you're at an advantage for this suspended variation. The "Vampire" gets its name from the fact that one of the participants hangs head down from the bar like a bat, while his partner stands upright in from of him, steering both boners into the appropriate places. Depending on how high the bar is, it can be a bit tricky to get both mouths and dicks at the same height. An adjustable stool can help. But once you've got all the parts aligned, the vampire can be a very stimulating position. The bat partner's hanging position means that every vibration is passed on through the bodies of both participants, and as both of them have their hands free,

there's a lot of leeway for extra caressing. Watch the Raging-Stallion porn movie *Behind the Big Top* for an impressive vampire performance by Jimmy Franz and Josh Long on a rope ladder. That should serve as the final proof that sucking dick is way better than sucking blood. By the way: hanging head down causes a rush of blood to the head. The hanging bat should make sure he doesn't get dizzy. So it's best to practice beforehand.

- Eight: Sideways
  After this acrobatic bat performance, I'm going to reward you with the most relaxed of all 69 positions. We're going to go back to bed, snuggle down into the pillows and do the simultaneous blow job on our sides. A pretty classic post-first-round exercise. Once you've released the first pent-up burst of desire, you can take your time to explore your lover's junk, untroubled by lust's impetuous commands—and after two minutes it's back in your mouth again, with the same thing happening on the other side of the mattress. Welcome to round two!

- Seven: Look, No Arms!
  We're going to stay lying down, but this time we'll add a challenge to our balancing skills. I'd even go so far as to say that the "Look, No Arms!" version of the 69 is more a game of skill than an erotic thrill, but that's a matter of opinion. It's all in the name: both lovers cross their arms behind their backs and get down to business. This isn't hard to do on your side, but if you're lying on top of each other, you need to compensate the lack of hands by bending your entire body. Unintentionally abrupt thrusts are a matter of course. But if you pick this method, the element of unpredictability is part of the game.

- Six: Standing Up
  Get out of bed and hit the floor. The standing 69 is the payback for the hanging 69. While the "vampire" entails greater difficulty and strain for the guy hanging upside down, this time it's the other way round. Instead of hanging from the horizontal bar,

one partner's entire weight is held in the arms of the partner standing upright, whom I'm going to call the load-bearer. He has to lift his partner up to his crotch to facilitate mutual sucking. Only men with very strong arms and a very strong back will be able to manage it. Proceed as follows: the upside down guy does a handstand and then lays his thighs over the shoulders of the load-bearer crouched in front of him. The latter then raises himself into a standing position and lifts his lover by the hips up to the required height. Differences in weight and size will simplify this procedure, but even then you'll only master this variation if you're acrobatically inclined.

- Five: The Two Piston Engine
Unlike its predecessor, this one is refreshingly simple! One guy lies flat on his back while his partner does a push-up over him. Two factors pose a challenge to the second guy's coordination skills: the dick in his mouth and the mouth sucking at his dick. This means that you can only blow and be blown with any depth if you go down really low. And you can only take this one to a happy ending if you can do push-ups really fast.

- Four: Sitting Down
A simple chair or armchair can make everything so much easier! Doing the 69 sitting down works the same way as doing it standing up, but it's not the same thing at all. This time, the guy standing up is the one sitting down, while the upside down partner is the one standing up. Not quite clear? The first guy sits down on a solid chair or armchair with his legs spread apart. The second guy does a headstand on the seat between his legs. And now, just hold onto each other, get your dicks in the right place, and hang in there.

- Three: The Seesaw
While the multi-tasking requirements of many variations on the 69 mean that there's often a lack of depth and thrust, this method should compensate for that. The seesaw is actually a standard 69

with two guys lying on top of each other, skin to skin. But the essential difference here is a simple rule that says: no sucking at the same time! Instead of simultaneous stimulation, you've got seamless alternation. Negotiate the duration beforehand. Within a single blow period lasting ten to twenty seconds, you can give it everything you've got and then have your partner give you everything right back. This position is less gentle, but interspersing breaks at regular intervals will help postpone your climax. The cute name originates in the upper partner's movements as he swings back and forth like a seesaw. Whenever it's his turn to suck, he'll raise his ass to keep his boner out of reach, and when it's his turn to get blown, he'll arch his back to keep himself out of temptation's reach. As your arousal increases, you can gradually shorten the blow periods.

- **Two: The Double Bridge**
  Remember the crab wanker in our masturbation chapter? The idea was to rub one out while doing the crab walk with one hand. We're going to be walking backwards on all fours again here. But this time, both feet stay on the ground. Because now, we've got another guy to bend over us and take care of our oral and genital needs. This position takes the singular bridge blow job to the plural 69. One guy sucks under the bridge, the other on the bridge. It's twice as hot.

- **One: The 69 Roll**
  This is just good clean fun. As a child, everyone has at one time or another tried to roll down a grassy or snowy slop and realized that the human form is not really made for rolling. But how about when two entwined bodies, locked in a 69, start to roll around, how does that work? I'll tell you: slowly. Every rotation becomes an achievement and every jolt becomes a challenge to your blow job skills. I don't need to tell you that you also have to keep your teeth under control. If you can do ten rolls and still be erect the whole time, then you're really rock-hard.

The Oral Office

The "Oral Office" is a gimmick position with a high potential for role-play. As most of you will have already guessed, the name refers to Bill Clinton's affair with his intern Monica Lewinksy in 1998. This

affair involved (ostensibly only) oral sex, giving the Oval Office its nickname, which it shares with this position—this being a pure and simple blow job under the desk. You don't really need instructions for this one, except perhaps for the guy under the table to mind his head so that he doesn't hit it while bobbing up and down. The whole thing can be dialed up a notch by including a third man carrying on a conversation with the guy being blown, without him letting on. If you're reached a certain level of arousal and you can't keep this game up, it's time to collectivize and move everything to the top of the desk, or underneath. Enact your own versions of what you think *really* happened in 1998.

The Statue

While you shouldn't do this to Michelangelo's *David*, you can go to town on a statue of flesh and blood. Take his dick in your mouth. You may not always be rewarded with greater measurements (according to my calculations, the monumental statue's member is only about 7 inches long—in relation to the rest of him, that's kind of disappointing), but definitely with a greater degree of gratitude. If you

want to stick to the sculptural motive, the guy giving the blow job can perform his task in the same pose as August Rodin's *Thinker*. And that's enough cultural references for today. The standing blow job position is called the "statue" because of its monolithic pose. Positioning yourself in the middle of the room means that the only thing the participants can hold onto is each other. This can be a really gripping affair once you start alternating the rhythm. But it's better to stay calm and enjoy. The guy performing the blow job can use one hand to direct his partner's dick or the massage his balls, while using the other to stroke his ass and his upper body. The other guy receives all this attention with trembling fortitude. And Michelangelo's *David* will go a mossy green with envy.

▶ **Crossing the Border**

A sliding door, a shower cubicle, a picket fence, a folding screen—this position's specialty consists first and foremost of its structural finesse. You need a gap wide enough for the guy giving the blow job to stick his head through, but no wider than shoulder breadth. The guy contributing his boner uses this gap to push his erect penis through and then leans both shoulders against it. The blow job giver approaches from the other side and greets the border crosser by licking him—and then using his greedy lips to suck him over to the other side. This almost allegorical position takes its attraction from the exciting interplay of intimacy and distance. On the one hand, the participants are very close to each other, on the other, they are both on different sides and can only "communicate" with each other through the gap. While both partners can move towards each other at the same time, creating the ultimate collision of lust, there's always the lingering fear of the other guy withdrawing and never returning. This position should be named the official position commemorating the fall of the Berlin Wall. Why am I saying "should"? Make it so! Meet you at the border! A simplified version of this method can also be done using a wire-mesh fence as a divider.

▶ **The Dead Man**

After the symbolic weight of Crossing the Border, it's time to lighten up again. So, off to bed and take up the position that follows this section's "Get Your Dick Out!" rule like no other: the Dead Man. The recipient lies on the bed with arms and legs stretched out (just as you do on the water's surface in the swim-

ming pool game of the same name) and lets his partner's resuscitation attempts get his juices flowing. The supreme command for the recipient is to remain passive. Like an animal offering up its throat to its opponent, he surrenders himself up. This makes him both his partner's prey and his most formidable opponent. The blow job giver needs to muster all his skills to work against his partner's deep relaxation. But that also gives him ample opportunity to showcase his art. As strength is born of peace, so is action born of passivity.

▶ Chinese De Luxe

I'd already mentioned that the mattress thrust is also known as the "Chinese Position" in our masturbation chapter. As well as the fact that the title refers to a practice originating in Great Britain. What I deliberately didn't mention was exactly how this is done. Because this one is a position in its own right. You'll need a bed slat without the mattress and a trestle or bed frame to put it on. It's important that the frame is high enough for a man to crawl under. Once there, he crouches patiently on the ground until another guy comes crawling over the bed slats and sticks his erect cock through the gap in the slats for a quick feed. Apparently, this is what the Chinese prostitutes who gave this position its name did in 19th century British opium dens. I hope they got something out of it. The sexual tension arising from the cage-like enclosure of the man under the slats, who at the same time has total control over depth and speed, has its own subtle attraction. So does thrusting through the wooden slats with your own wood. Chinese is back in fashion.

▼ Open Up!

▷ Mouth-Fucking

Say "Ah"! For a mouth fuck, the blow job giver just opens up his mouth and waits to be fed. You can do that in any position, but to really do justice to the name, perform this position lying down. That way, the top can mount the guy below him and ram his boner down his throat, just like it was his ass. If you thrust hard enough, you won't hear another "Ah," just a breathless panting and gurgling. As it's difficult to express yourself verbally with your mouth full, you should agree on a manual signal beforehand, so that the guy on the bottom can call a halt to the proceedings if necessary.

▷ The Crab Thrust

I always deliver on my promises. Following the Crab Wanker and the 69 Double Bridge, we're going to return to the backwards crab walk once more. But this time we're going to invite our eager partners crouching down between our legs to a meal. The propped up crab position presents the blow job giver with kind of a dining table, where a fresh and juicy dick awaits him. But fresh doesn't mean overripe. To enhance this position's ritual attraction, have your guest lick his candy bar until it's stiff before devouring it. The ensuing pumping action is a great hip workout for the crab, but it's also suitable for blow job beginners: the recipient has only a limited range of movement, preventing any excessively hard pounding.

▷ The Neck Brace

When tenderness goes hand in hand with harshness and a choking grip triggers anticipation instead of terror, then you're in the neck brace position. The recipient sits on the edge of a chair or the couch with one foot on the ground and the other placed on his knee, forming a triangle between his calf and both thighs. The blow job giver then sticks his head up through this triangle from below. From this point, there's an entire playground of opportunities on offer. The closeness and intimacy of the neck brace effect created by the bent leg can be increased or decreased at will, using leverage. Opening up your leg will loosen your hold, but if you pull your raised foot further up towards your body, you will also tighten the noose around your partner's neck, pushing his nose into the shaft of your cock. Or his lips into your balls. Or his forehead against your glans. Once your penis has been swallowed, you can also use this thigh lever to regulate the rhythm.

▶ The Melon Head

If you're not keen on the mess of fucking a melon but would still like to sample some of its benefits, just do it with a partner—who is generally the object of your desire anyway, for which a punctured piece of fruit is only a poor substitute. To be precise, the Melon Head is merely an upright version of the Mouth Fuck, or a more gripping version of the Statue. But this method is so much fun, I thought I'd give it its own paragraph. If you've ever stood over your lover and, taking hold of his ears, pushed him over genitals, I'm sure you'll agree. And if you've ever taken your lover's head in both hands and pressed it into your loins, you'll agree with me too. And if you've ever caught sight of the famous blow job look (from below, and with a full mouth), then I don't have to convince you of the outstanding qualities of this position. One melon, please!

▶ The Second Floor

Give your blow job a double floor simply by climbing onto a chair. Squat down on the seat and lure your partner kneeling on the ground to you by wagging your dick back and forth at him. It won't take long for him to take the bait. Then you can go from gentle to rough. The guy on his knees can duck down between his partner's legs and pinch his nipples according to taste, while man upstairs can rhythmically pump his pelvis up and down or even grab hold of the other guy's head with his legs. Once he's in the pincer hold, all the man downstairs can do is swallow. This way, you can also turn this upstairs/downstairs constellation into a stylized depiction of dominance and submission. But while only the toughest will be able to keep up this position for long, it really works your thighs. And here's another tip: please try this out on a solidly built chair, otherwise you might loosen the joins in the heat of the moment and your session will come to an abrupt end with a dive headfirst into the ground floor. I know what I'm talking about here. You can use an armchair for a more comfortable version, or a revolving office chair to test your balance.

▶ **The Figurehead**

A ship, its figurehead, and the infinite ocean of foreplay. These three romantic elements make up the following position, with the blow job giver lying flat on the bed, representing the ship's hull, and the obligatory nude figurehead plugged in at the bow: the top. He kneels over the lower guy's chest with his erection inserted into his partner's porthole (mouth). Before I let my seaman's (heh) vocabulary get away with me, I'd better just say: anchors away and full speed ahead! Let the figurehead lean into the rough seas and slide back and forth in its anchoring and the foaming surf. A stormy affair, with the risk of being shipwrecked on board all the while. Ahoy!

Ball Licking—It's an Art

Guilty as charged. I have not hitherto really gone into orally servicing the testicles. A grievous lapse, you might think, but it isn't. Because the omission of any reference to licking balls and the inclusion of this info-box have one and the same cause, which may be summarized as follows. In the context of the positions we have described, ball licking is, due to its lack of relevance to the "main program" at hand, merely a bonus option. Admittedly, I could have duly mentioned this practice as such. I have not done so because I assumed that any dedicated blow job giver will have already included his lover's nuts in the demonstration of his skills, without being explicitly told to. And I also belive that to reduce ball licking to a mere side attraction would be to sorely trivialize the attendant risks and opportunities. This practice is an art in its own right. There's a whole lot you can do wrong, but then there's also a whole lot you can do right. Instead of treating it in an incidental aside, I therefore give you the following seven virtues and deadly sins of ball licking. Often enough, they are the two sides of the same coin.

- **One: Forgetting!** The preservation of my honor is also the preservation of your reputation as a lover. If you forget about the balls when you're performing oral sex, you're missing out on a variety of opportunities. But hopefully, thanks to this special section, this won't ever happen to you. And now for the technique.

- **Two: Looking!** Scrota are like dicks—no two are the same. Before you start nibbling at them, you should take a good look. Is this a smaller specimen that shrinks at the lightest touch? Or is it a low-hanging moneybag, drawn out by the sheer weight of its contents? There are many nuances in between. A very approximate rule of thumb on how to proceed with sac-sucking is: the smaller the sac, the more care you should take in handling it.

- **Three: Blowing!** Running the entire breadth of your tongue over the scrotum and then blowing on it is the ball licker's litmus test. Your partner's reaction will immediately tell you whether or not he's into testicle treatment. A negative reaction may however stem just as much from oversensitivity due to a lack of experience. So if it's not just a one night stand, keep it up and try to push his tolerance levels.

- **Four: Pulling!** If you haven't got a moneybag dangling in front of you, you won't be able to dispense with this. That actually goes for everyone else, too. Pull his nuts down with a ring formed by your thumb and index finger and flick your tongue over the taut skin. This will generally be rewarded.

- **Five: Swallowing!** Now it's time to ramp up the action. Once you've stretched his balls, the next logical step is to take them into your mouth. There's always the risk of his balls slipping apart uncontrollably, which can cause their owner pain. So here's my tip: first suck each ball singly. If you're going to swallow them together, make sure your lips form a cuff above them (like the thumb-and-finger-ring) to prevent slippage. As a rule: sucking is fine, pulling is not. If you're not involved with an experienced ballbusting fetishist, always exercise restraint when sucking on his balls. We can compare this to walking a dog: you should always make sure the leash is never completely taut, it should always have some slack.

- **Six: Biting!** Incredibly hot, but difficult. There is always the risk of slipping off. In this case, biting is more a form of sucking while occasionally incorporating a chewing motion. Any attempt to pull one or even both testicles away from the body between your teeth, is almost always doomed to failure. A better method is to carefully squeeze them between your teeth and your tongue.

- **Seven: Shaving!** This issue will crop up again and again: you're into licking balls, but you're less into hairs in your mouth. An unshaven date leaves you with three options: leave out the ball licking, open up and think of England, or offer your services. The latter means: shaving as sex play. If you're well-practiced (this includes shaving your own sac) and not under time pressure, you can go ahead and make an offer. It's a lot of fun and great for creating a playful sense of intimacy. But if you've never shaved anyone's pubes before, skip this part. You can't just attack a guy's crown jewels with a razor without any previous experience. And one more thing: many men will feel sore right after shaving. So don't get pissed off if your plan backfires on you.

▼ Eat Ass!

▶ Facesitting

Take a seat ... and sex! There's not much more you need to say about a position where one guy spreads his cheeks and sits down on his partner's face, is there? Welcome to the ass-eating department. Anilingus (derived from the Latin anus—"asshole" and lingere—"to lick") has a rather dubious reputation, due in part to the fact that it was used in the Middle Ages as a device for humiliation—from where we get the expression "kiss my ass." Anilingus has always played a role in sexual activity, and it has always been taboo, something that also plays a role in the exclusion of gay sexuality in the media.

But now for the practical part: your Average Joe will probably be familiar with facesitting in its more moderate form, where the recipient doesn't really sit on his partner's face but merely squats

over him invitingly, letting him flick his tongue over his sphincter. Kinksters will also be familiar with any number of hardcore versions—from underwater sex with breath play elements to scat play. Hardened facesitters will plant their rear ends on padded smother boxes. You could describe these gadgets as something like a miniature privy, which the licker then sticks his head into in order to pleasure his partner's crack through a hole in the lid. As the name suggests, breath play is often included. And now I've gone on for far too long about a position that doesn't really need explaining. Just try it out!

▶ The Joystick

The guy underneath can lie on the ground, the bed, or the lawn, while his partner turns his back to him, kneels on his chest, and offers up his butt. As this position is a first-rate starting point for a 69, there's a tendency to skip ahead and not to linger on its own merits. The basic position and its name are more or less self-explanatory.

But if you want the details: the guy lying down has a butt in front of his face, which he can warm up by licking, kissing, and taking tiny bites. The guy kneeling on top of him has an excellent view of his crotch, which at this point will probably already be sporting a large and healthy boner: the joystick. The chest rider grabs hold of this. And that's the go-ahead for the rimming-wanking-challenge, where both players adjust the force of their tongue thrusts and dick massaging to signalize to their partners when it's time to speed things up or to take things down a notch. It's a great opportunity to practice your non-verbal communication skills and to learn to read your partner's body language.

▶ Sloth Style

To get the most out of your monkey bar, I'm going to go back to a suspended rimming position that I first saw in the Naked Sword porn movie *The Mix*. Connor Maguire and Conner Habib do a really hot trick in the woods, where the foreplay includes a sequence in which Conner Habib hangs from a branch, sloth style, his colleague standing below him, supporting him with his hands and rimming him at the same time. It looks absolutely spectacular and I simply had to try it out. And wouldn't you know it: to my surprise, it wasn't that difficult. Once you're hanging there with your feet hooked behind the bar, it's still quite a strain on your hands and arms, but as you've got an assistant holding you, a lot of the strain is passed over to him—which I experienced firsthand when we switched roles. I'll be frank with you: I'm just too lazy to hold and lick at the same time. I'd rather be the sloth.

▶ The 96

After our extensive ten point disquisition on the 69 position, the name of this position more or less answers any question you might have. I've got to admit though, I'm cheating a bit here. Strictly speaking, the opening of the nine should be facing the six, if you want to depict the bodies' positions correctly. But that would mean turning the nine around, and then it wouldn't be a nine, it would be some nonexistent digit. So let's not ask what's in a name and just concentrate on the only position that makes sense of the 96 in a rimming contect: two naked bodies on top of each other, with the upper guy's butt aligned with the lower guy's face for easy rimming access. I might also mention that you can try out this position while sitting down, standing up, hanging from a bar and rolling around. But let's be honest: unlike the 69, this position has fixed top and bottom roles which makes interpreting it in different ways rather less exciting.

▷ Diving off a Cliff

Build up the suspense till the first flick of the tongue! This experiment starts out with the recipient straddling the tongue artist lying beneath him. He then descends into a squatting position, lowering his rear end over his lover's face. He can hold on to the other guy's bent knees while doing this. The more slowly you lower your butt, the more exciting it is for your partner, who can watch your open hole slowly approaching him. If it looks like it's about to float past his tongue, he can steer it back on track with his hands. The rest is precision plugging, the likes of which you'll only see in high-precision construction. This practice takes its name from the high degree of suspense it arouses. Lowering your anus back towards your lover's tongue is like jumping off a cliff at night. You never know when exactly you're going to touch the water's surface, or in this case, the tip of his tongue. The ensuing rimming session can be extremely hard work for the guy on top. I strongly advise stopping by the sex gym first—focusing on the Penis Raise and the Male Quadriga.

▷ The Anvil

An anvil is usually used to beat heated iron on. So what better metaphor for an experienced male butt, which also longs for the ardor of red-hot iron? In other words: this is for the more advanced rimmers out there.

It's not for nothing that this position is also a first rate preparation for the previously mentioned Pile Driver.

Let's proceed: the rim job recipient lifts himself up from the ground into the candle pose, bends his legs, and spreads them so that they form a triangle above his body. This creates an outline that gives the position its name. Anvils generally have two lateral wings standing out from the face, which creates the characteristic triangle shape. But whereas in metalworking the attendant sounds are caused by horseshoes and iron bars, in this case, the cause is the sturdy thrusts of the analinguist's toungue. In the standard version, the rimmer will kneel down in front of his anal anvil, warm the orifice up with a couple of licks, and then penetrate it with the tip of his tongue, now stiffened to a point, in a hard staccato rhythm. For a more hardcore version, the tongue artist can reach his lower arms underneath the leg triangle and lift the entire anvil up. While standing, he'll hand-bang his way into the other guy's hole

The more tender souls among us will have to go and lie down for a while after this, but others, more hardened, will be greedily antici-pating the main attraction. Or how does the Italian figure of speech put it? "A good anvil does not fear the hammer." And neither do we.

▶ **Anal Backward Roll**

The Anal Backward Roll is simply the Somersault Shot with good company. You assume the candle pose and lower your legs down over your head, and then you call your stud over to take care of your hole. If he's really good, he can massage your boner at the same time; that way you won't have to do anything but tie yourself in knots and enjoy. But you know the dangers of idleness. You only get ideas. Supercock Steve Stiffer must have thought the same thing when he nonchalantly combined the Anal Backwards Roll with a spot of autofellatio in the Falcon porn movie *Rub Me Right.*

Rimming—Playing Dirty?

There's body shaving, there's anal bleaching, there's muscle implants, but a solution for shit, there is not. Apart from fasting that is, and let's be straight here: starving yourself so you can stay clean for sex—that's taking it too far in my opinion. Although I do realize that a lot of people do it. But in my case, it's just counter productive. Being hungry lowers my energy levels, which then lowers my interest in sex, and if I have no interest in sex, then there's no reason for me to starve myself. So I just eat normally. Apart from that, there are a couple of methods out there to minimize the risk of a disastrous accident.

Before I go into these, just let me say this: you really need to lighten up a bit, people. I don't know anyone with even a moderately fulfilled sex life who hasn't had some kind of accident involving shit while doing anal. Of course it's not very nice. And if I walk through a darkroom straight into a horrible stinking cloud then, no, that does not turn me on. Neither does entering a fuck cubicle, only to find a couple of wipes stinking the place up. Or realizing I've hit dirt while fucking. I also know how embarassing it can be for a bottom to suddenly realize he's had a terrible mishap. All of this is truly horrible, but getting upset won't clean the mess up and, unless that's been agreed upon beforehand, nobody will have done it on purpose. In addition, this kind of thing happens more frequently if you let yourself be overcome by lust or if you let your partner talk you into going farther than you had originally intended. Listening to your body and its needs and current states is the most reliable "protection" of all. In this context, condoms can also be a great aid to hygiene. And a little preparation doesn't hurt, either.

- **An anal douche:** This is a lifetime investment. If you've installed an anal douche system in your bathroom, you're that much closer to rectal cleanliness—especially psychologically. Normally, your intestine should have cleaned itself within two hours after your last visit to the bathroom, but as most people find it difficult to rely on this, a quick douche with a dildo nozzle is a gentle and, at least with respect to your rectum, effective method. Always use lukewarm water, otherwise you'll get cramps. And let's be absolutely clear on this: anal douches should only be used for cleansing purposes. Do not keep the water in your ass. That's what an enema is for.

- **Enemas:** If you have greater ambitions regarding dick size or dimensions, treat yourself to a disposable enema from the drugstore three hours before you start. This will give you a deep cleanse. Use this to squirt a saline solution into your ass and keep it there for up to ten minutes. Then "spit it out" into the toilet. The saline solution has cleansing properties, but it is also a laxative. You shouldn't use it more than twice a week. Disposable units aside, you can also get reusable enemas which you should fill with water.

- **Syringes and others:** For an alternative to anal douching, use a simple hypodermic syringe without the needle. Cyclists' water bottles with a stopper also work amazingly well. Just fill it up with lukewarm water, squeeze some of it (200 ml are sufficient) into your anus and squirt it out again into the toilet. Repeat until the water runs out clear.

- **Laxatives:** These compounds are designed to facilitate bowel movements and are hailed by many an anal adept as a miracle cure. That's bullshit. This stuff is formulated to combat constipation and that's what it should be used for. If you're healthy, it will emaciate your body rather than keep it permanently clean.

Cowboy, Surfboard, Doggy Style: Positions for Anal Sex

Finally! It's time to fuck. This means an immeasurable increase in the number of possible bodily configurations and will also show whether the lessons learned in the previous chapters have borne fruit. The attentive student of the *Gayma Sutra* will have already noticed that certain elements crop up over and over again and that some methods are simply adapted to suit the respective topics. The core lesson here is that you can rediscover them again and again, a lesson that you will also hopefully be able to apply to your own love life. Aptly enough, the following chapter will focus more strongly on the lessons of the original *Kama Sutra*, even though anal intercourse barely plays a role there. There is a reference to "adhorata"–the "love of the nether hole"–but this is a largely derided custom "prevalent among the people of the South." In solidarity with these people, I shall be shifting some of the *Kama Sutra* positions from the upper hole to the nether one. But only the amusing ones. After all, there are plenty of gay originals to be taken into account. Just as in the oral sex chapter, I've sorted everything into categories of top and bottom dominance–but this time I'll be using the simple slogans "In!" (dick) and "Out!" (ass). The final "In-Out!" section features the three best positions in which both roles are equally dominant.

So, have fun stuffing and offering up your nether holes.

▼ In!

▷ The Missionary—Top Ten

The sections of this chapter will also start off with a classic position which can be adapted in many different ways. I've already gone into the practice, name, and benefits of the missionary position (bottom lies on his back with his legs bent / top mounts him face to face) in the chapter on what the pros are doing, which is why I'll be following the familiar the top-ten-list-method to highlight the best and gayest aspects of this legendary position.

- **Ten: On the Edge of the Bed**
  Due to the nature of this position, the gay version of the heterosexual original presents more difficulties with regard to the accuracy of anatomical fit. A straight guy can just shove his thing straight in from above, while most gay studs are faced with an insertion angle that's just a bit steeper than it should be ideally. This means that the top always has to "duck down" a bit, or else ask the bottom to raise his ass a little. You can avoid this problem by relocating the action from the bed's center to the edge. The bottom should scoot his ass just over the edge of the mattress and that way the stud can find the ideal angle for insertion from a standing position. This saves you from bending too far, without losing any of the face to face benefits of this position.

- **Nine: Hand in Hand**
  A big part of the missionary position's popularity is the romantic aspect of being able to make eye contact while you're fucking. You can enhance this emotional effect even more by holding hands while getting it on. Just place your palms together and lock fingers. This will accentuate and intensify the sensation of physical attachment.

- **Eight: The Tailbone Curl**
  For a more comfortable alternative to the edge of the bed, prop up the bottom's ass by placing a large pillow or rolled-up blanket underneath. This raised position makes insertion easier for the top, and the slight incline also allows him to increase the pressure of his thrusts.

- **Seven: The Splits**
  It's time for the guy underneath to stretch his legs out and spread them wide! Your goal is not to do a full gymnast's split (but you

can always try), but to allow your stud to grab your legs at the ankles or around the calves and use them as a supporting lever to deliver a powerful salvo.

- **Six: The Car Jack**
  Following the same principle as the penis raise, the top can also lift his partner's body up with the power of his erection. This should be tried out on the edge of the bed and it definitely shouldn't be taken absolutely literally. The bottom does need to help the top out a little to prevent any mishap, strain, or the entire session grinding to a halt. Cheating a little together will only increase your erotic bond, and you both get to enjoy the feeling of triumph together once you've made it.

- **Five: The Crane**
  Adapted from the original *Kama Sutra*, with the bottom's legs wrapped tightly around the top's hips. Unlike the Indrani position

(see the "Out!" section), this entwining isn't a means of control, but rather an invitation to increase the force of his thrusts. You can also drum your heels on your lover's rump. This is especially effective if he pushes his cock in up to the hilt and then pauses for a second, allowing both partners to feel the muffled vibrations.

- Four: The Push-up Missionary
  No basic position would be complete with an athletic variation. The Push-up Missionary is just a bit of fun, where the top inserts his wang with a push-up movement instead of thrusting his hips. He should use both hands to support himself on the bottom's thighs. This is best done on the edge of the bed.

- Three: The Leg-up
  You should definitely do this one on the edge of the bed. The Leg-up is actually a position in its own right, but its face-to-face qualities have earned it a place in the missionary family. The bottom scoots his butt up a bit further over the edge of the mattress, so that the top can push both hands under his rear end and lift him up if necessary. This will give you a nice, compact fucking position which also gives the bottom the snug sensation of being held as well as pounded.

- Two: Boccie Balls
  I already mentioned the Boccie Ball position in our discussion of accidental discoveries. While trying these positions out, I instinctively tried to think about what the reverse of each position might be. Lying on your back/on your front, from behind/the front, lying down/standing up ... that kind of thing. The boccie balls resulted from the missionary splits as described in point seven. According to the basic principle of "if you can spread it, you can close it up again," I tried closing my legs and discovered the resulting fucking position: nice and tight, lacking the much-vaunted eye contact (your view is blocked by your clenched knees), but giving you the option of wedging your balls between your legs, so that

the top bumps into them gently at every thrust. A very nice bonus that more than compensates for the lack of eye contact.

- **One: The Cradle**
  Letting himself flop forwards once he's plugged in and propping himself up on his hands on either side of the bottom's chest brings the top especially close to his partner and also allows him to stretch one leg out behind him and move it up and down. This rocking motion automatically propels his dick in and out of his partner's hole, a movement that the top can intensify by rocking his upper body at the same time. Use the latter movement as a great kissing opportunity. The cradle is more of a position for intimate enjoyment than breathless shagging, anyway.

▶ **The Helicopter**

With the bottom playing the role of the cabin and the top as the propeller, the helicopter is a spectacular sight. Davey Wavey's video *Creative Sex Positions* offers a visual sample of what it means to

spin like a rotor blade on your partner's ass. Only in this video, the protagonists keep their shorts on, so they aren't really rotating their boners in their partner's anus like an axle bearing.

And they presumably know why. The helicopter sounds great in theory, but once you try and put it into practice, you'll be brought up short by the limitations of human anatomy. But let's take it one step at a time. The principle is just easy to explain as it is hard to carry out: the bottom takes up the somersault shot position on the ground and the top inserts his boner into his hole from above. Then he does his best airplane impression. In this case, this means he takes his feet off the ground, stretches out his arms, and balances in mid-air, anchored only by his dick-plug in his partner's ass. Seen from the side, this might look a bit like the famous dance lift in *Dirty Dancing*, except with the pedastal formed not by a pair of outstretched arms but by an anal backward roll.

I say "might" and that's just what I mean. Because this doesn't actually work without the airplane guy tipping over to the front. Over and over again. Without fail. At least, that was my personal experience. I would give you an account of all the unedifying details, but there simply isn't enough space (after all, I wasn't the only person concerned, the other test subject—the bottom—foundered pretty soon as well), and so I'll skip straight to my proposed solutions. These being a chair circle or a third man. Regarding the former: if you place a circle of chairs around the anal helicopter cabin for the propellor guy to hold on to and pull himself around in a circle, you could theoretically make it work. But as you can probably imagine, this is an extremely awkward solution and it won't make the project take off. But as regards the third man: if he holds on to the propellor guy's wrists and pushes him around in a circle, that might work as well. On the other hand, that's closer to a pony ride on a lunge rein than a rapid fuck-flight. And so we proceed to point three: the bottom's role should only be taken on by a real expert. Your ass funnel isn't an axle bearing and an erect dick just doesn't revolve in a perfect circle. I went through four test subjects (myself included) before managing to complete a single cycle. By then, we'd already spent any amount of sweat, lube, and tears of laughter. So that's enough talk about an impossible position, although in theory, I still think it's great.

▶ Leapfrog

While a certain degree of instability is an abiding feature of most standing positions, the Leapfrog position is literally down-to-earth. As I mentioned before, I came across this position more or less by accident. My ex and I were actually trying out one of the variations on the 69 positions, where the guy in front bends down, supporting himself with his hands on this shins, while the other guy penetrates him from behind. So, nothing spectacular. Our field studies however showed that while being relatively uncomfortable and wobbly, you could compensate for this position's lack of stability by having the guy in front (in this case, me) lean back a little. We went on fooling around for a while, and as I was still standing bent over, my partner

leapfrogged over my back. This immediately provided us with the groundwork for a new position—based on the vaulting horse used in gymnastics. The horse has four legs, and so does the leapfrog. Just stand with your legs apart, lean forward until you land on all fours and wait for your partner to penetrate you from behind. Not a wobble in sight—and by standing with your legs apart, you make it easier for your partner to come up behind you and plug himself in. To my taste, this version is much better than the one where you hold onto your shins. But don't take my word for it—try it out yourself.

▶ The Fuckquake

Speaking of positions with parts held in mid-air, there's another option for the bottom to just let it all hang. But this one is slightly less comfortable. To do the fuckquake, the bottom supports himself on the edge of a couch, table, or window ledge behind him. Then his partner pulls his legs away from under him and drapes them over his arms. This results in the following: the bottom's ass hangs in mid-air, with the backs of his kness hooked over the crook of his partner's arms so that his hands reaching back are the only point of contact with a solid surface. You can imagine what happens next: the stud has to lunge out and drive his member into the swinging ass in front of him. And then you go hog wild. This finally provides the somewhat overblown literary motive of bodies "quaking" with a physical equivalent. As there's nothing to absorb the force of the top's thrusts, every vibration will make its way through the bodies of the protagonists. Depending on how hard you pound, your partner's in for quite a shaking. And that's the fuckquake. At least five points on the Richter scale.

▶ The Shadow Thrust

Peter Pan lost his shadow, we're going to let it fuck us. The title of this position refers to the synchronicity of the partners involved and to the top standing in the bottom's shadow. In other words, coming up from behind. Here's the setup: the recipient lies on his side with his lower leg stretched out and the upper leg raised at an angle. The *Kama Sutra* would call this position the "Half Press," but we don't have time for that now. Because there's a shadow creeping up behind the unsuspecting sphinx lying spreadeagled on the bed. And before you know it, he's plunged its hard rod into his ass. His legs take up the same position as the sphinx. And now it's time to make a date with the dark side ... and if you strip away all the purple prose I've decked this description with, you'll be left with the part that makes this position a memorable experience: the shadow thrust. Despite the lack of eye contact, this position is great for intimacy, as you can latch on from behind with plenty of skin contact and then wrap your arms around the guy in front of you.

▷ The Right Angle

The Right Angle fuck offers you the opportunity to literally get to know your partner's dick from another angle. And it's a first rate example for the enormous effect the tiniest shift can have. The bottom lies on the bed with his legs bent. The tops lies down right behind them, so that their bodies are at a right angle. Seen from above, they look like an upside down "T." The interesting part of fucking in this position is penetrating at an unfamiliar angle. Especially tops with a markedly curved boner will notice the difference—as, of course, will the bottom.

That way, both partners profit from a shift in the fucking axis. The bottom can spread or clench his thighs, contracting his sphincter muscles for a more intense experience.

▶ The Taskmaster

Sometimes you can be dominant by not doing anything at all. The taskmaster position is ideal for this. But you can also do the reverse: demanding constant, merciless action. In this position, the principle of surrender plays a subtle but essential role. The initial setup says it all, really. The bottoms squats on the bed with his legs apart, supporting himself on his outstretched arms, while the top kneels behind him with his dick in his ass, casually leaning back on the edge of the bed. Will he start pounding him? Or will he tenderly rub the shoulders of the man in front of him? Or will he give the order to start circling his hips? The lure of the unpredictable is what makes this position so special. It's softcore S/M, without all the gadgets. The bottom surrenders himself up to the top's will—squatting down, with his ass cheeks spread and with his

hole penetrated by the top's dick. He knows full well that all hell is about to break loose in his rectal cavity. But when? Only the task-master knows, and he gets off on letting him sweat a little. Well, perhaps it *is* hardcore after all.

▼ Out!

▷ The Cowboy—Top Ten

The cowboy position is every power bottom's all time favorite. This makes sense on all counts. First of all, the cowboy has always been a recurring motif in homoerotic fantasies, secondly, he's fully in command of his mount instead of the horse never commanding him. All in all, it's a great metaphor for our next section "Out!" The

name refers not to submissively sticking out your ass but rather to its unashamedly demanding counterpart. It's time for the bottoms to call the shots. In the case of the cowboy position, they do this by first of all mounting their steeds. Cowboy positions mean the top's on the bottom and the bottom's on top. The former lies stretched out with the other guy sitting on his lap. The bottom rides his top, the top gets ridden, and there's plenty of ways to do it. Here are the top ten:

- Ten: The Frontal Cowboy
  Kneeling on your lover's lap, riding him, and watching his face as you grind him ... there really is nothing better. Beginners and couples in the first stages of a relationship might want to start out with the basic cowboy position. Not necessarily because it's more fun that way, but because it's a great way to get to know each other. Your partner's reactions to having his dick ridden will tell you a lot about his experience, temperament, and ability to enjoy himself—and help you predict what your future sex life will be like. A guy who keeps trying to thrust from below is just a macho who will never understand that a top can be passive too. A guy who appears tense and obviously overwhelmed by a rectal ride but doesn't complain may be inexperienced, but he'll learn. A guy who just leans back and leaves all the work to you is capable of enjoying himself but he'll always be a lazy lover. And a guy who watches you in action, occasionally telling you whenever he wants it slower, faster, or just like that, is a real stroke of luck, as he sees sex as the form of communication that it really is. The frontal cowboy is a great opportunity to learn these lessons, and many more. But now it's time to turn our backs on him. Or his on us.

- Nine: The Reverse Cowboy
  As before, the cowboy sits on the other guy's dick, but this time facing the other way. It's not always easy to keep the tension going in this position. If the lack of both eye contact and an equal division of labor leads to both partners feeling isolated, that

doesn't do erotic harmony any good. But you can help combat this tendency towards isolation by caressing each other above and beyond your coupled parts. The guy underneath can stroke the rider's back, while the rider strokes his legs. In any case: it's an ass-tronomical sensation, which the cowboy can enhance even further by leaning forwards or backwards slightly.

- Eight: The Drawbar
  Sticking with the reverse position, we're going to liven it up a little. The top draws his legs towards him and holds up his calves like a drawbar. Now there's love for you. The cowboy can grab hold of his ankles and use them to pull himself vigorously onto his partner's lap. This truly has an in-depth appeal.

- Seven: Supported Cowboy
  The guy underneath spreads his legs again, but this time he places his feet on the mattress with the jockey crouching between them. With the other guy's dick plugged in, of course. The latter is then pushed up and down the cowboy's sphincter while he pushes himself up and down, holding on to the top's knees for support. His legs should be squeezed tightly together, so that he can rub his own boner between his thighs.

- Six: Pegasus
  Even a cowboy needs a break from being dominant now and then. That's what the Pegasus position is for, where the rider leans back, propping himself up with his arms, and lets his mighty steed flap his wings—that is to say, pound him from below—for a few precious minutes.

- Five: Rodeo
  A hook securely attached to the ceiling, the bars of a loft bed or the aforementioned monkey bar—all of these can facilitate what the riding community calls the "hanging cowboy." The diabolically dominant bottom attaches a noose above his ride and during the course of the ensuing fuck-rodeo, uses it to hold onto, pull

himself up, or even swing back and forth. This fun and energetic position will goad you on to more extreme moves. Please don't fall off and don't forget the subtler moves. Going up and down in slow motion will provide a real thrill for both partners.

- Four: Sidesaddle

  In the purely equestrian arts, this is the ladies' position, but in our case, it's for gentlemen only. I'm referring to sitting down sideways. By changing the curve and angle of the penis entering the anal cavity, it stimulates entirely new regions. For even more variation, I would recommend switching sides in the same session. If the stud can take it, try switching sides without dismounting.

- Three: Extended

  And now we'll turn to face our stallion again. While sitting on his dick, extend your legs out to the front and hook your feet behind his head. Then do slow reverse push-ups on his pelvis. Hold his gaze and don't give him his head. Hot!

- Two: Equestrian Vaulting

  After all this riding experience, you might want to master a few tricks. Switching sides in the sidesaddle position is good practice—and now you can try an entire cycle—as compensation for screwing up the helicopter. And what do you know: rotating is a lot easier in the cowboy position. Do it slowly and watch out for the top's dick, but vaulting isn't the same as flying, anyway.

- One: The Mute Toad

  Now you can demonstrate what you've learned during the big Kegel and its reverse equivalent. To do the "mute toad," return to the frontal position (try squatting instead of kneeling) and do … nothing! At least, that's what it might look like—if it weren't for your steed's twitching mouth and labored breathing. Because you're rewarding him for his services with a luxurious anal massage. Ribbit!

▶ **The Sailing Cruise**

Prepare with these five steps! First: the bottom lies down on his back. Second: he bends his right leg at the knee. Third: twisting his hips slightly, he moves his angled leg over to the left. Four: the top kneels behind his partner, with his partner's extended left leg between his own legs and the other leg wrapped around his right thigh. Five: Penetration! That was the preparatory phase and now it's time to set sail. The bottom's cocked leg acts as a sort of railing for the top while the bottom uses it as a tiller. For the non-nautically inclined: the tiller is the long lever on a sailboat that is used to steer. I've used this term because the bottom's angled leg acts as a steering element. By extending it, he can make the man behind slow down or even throw him off. He can also draw it up even further to draw him deeper inside him.

▶ The Indrani Position

This is another position taken from the original *Kama Sutra*. The bottom lies on his back with his legs bent and slightly spread. While his partner penetrates him, he hooks his feet into the top's armpits. If you've been reading closely, you'll have noticed something: this is actually a variation on the missionary position. That's true. But in this case (unlike the missionary), the bottom uses his legs to steer, which plays an important role in this position, warranting its inclusion in the "Out!" section of this chapter. The Indrani position get its name from the Vedic divinity Indra, and it provides the bottom with a good many opportunities to pull his partner towards him or to push him away. The bottom can switch from hooking his feet under his partner's armpits to wrapping his legs around the top's hips. Bracing his feet against the top's chest provides him with resistance or he can reach up with his hands, which usually lie beside his body to set the rhythm. But the best part is when both partners are in harmony and the top rests his entire weight on his partner's butt without being told to do so. This is the ultimate bonding sensation. Sound a bit cheesy? Blame it on Indra's influence. The god of fertility and rain is the embodiment of the grand gesture. Which is why he is the proud owner of one hundred (!) testicles.

▶ The Jockey

This tricky mid-air position is a very acrobatic form of surrender. The top sits on a chair while the bottom turns his back on him and sits on his lap, then the top inserts his dick into his partner's anus. So far, so good. But the Derby is yet to begin. The race starts the moment the bottom places both wrists behind his back for the guy sitting down to take hold. Once he has done so, the bottom leans forward, folds his lower legs up and jams his feet behind the back of the chair. And they both set off on a very strange ride, in which their respective roles blur into one another. On the one hand, the lap-sitter is the jockey, riding the man underneath him, on the other, it's the guy sitting down, holding his partner's wrists in his hands like reins.

This position makes jockeys of us all. But the great thing about it is the way it demonstrates the power of trust. Jockey number one has to hold onto jockey number two to prevent him falling from the saddle. To do this takes not only strength, but also integrity. Both qualities generally play an important role for really good sex and this is the ideal position for testing them.

▷ Little Dipper

Our chapter on what the pros are doing introduced us to a man who calls himself Big Dipper, without having ever tried out the position of the same name. Most likely because it's too strenuous. So here's a slightly less demanding (at least for the tops) alternative: the Little Dipper. As a quick reminder: the Little Dipper's big brother involves supporting yourself with your hands on the seat of a couch, placing your feet on a footstool and doing reverse push-ups. Each push-up has the wonderful effect of the athlete not only raising his own body, but also driving his dick into the hole of his partner standing over him. This holy alliance of fitness and sexual benefits is also a characteristic of the Little Dipper.

It even uses the same push-up technique. This time however, you switch roles. Now the bottom has to push himself up and down—and by doing so, ram his asshole over his lazy lover's dick with every downward movement.

▷ The Surfboard

A board in bed? No, you don't want that. But how about an inclined board? A surfboard, to be precise. A surfboard with a passenger waiting for the perfect orgasmic wave ... OK, sorry, got carried away there. Let's start over: for this position, the top forms a bridge with his body between the ground and a chair, and his calves lying on the seat. A classic planking position in other words. However, you need to hold this position for longer than a quick snapshot, long enough for the aforementioned orgasmic wave to come roaring up. And all this with a lust-riding surfer on your loins, fimly anchored to his board by his boner. I don't need to tell you that all this is very hard work, right? While the bottom can hold onto his animated surfboard's shins and enjoy the benefits of the unusually steep penetration angle in his anus, the top has to hold onto one thing only: body tension, body tension, body tension. You'd really have to love your bottom to put yourself through all this strain for his sake. And

he'd better love you back for it. You could almost turn this into a heart position.

But it's just too strenuous for me.

▶ **The Trailer**

If you've got two guys going in opposite directions but both of them with the same goal, they're probably doing the trailer position. This is the logical continuation of the anal backward roll. The bottom assumes the somersault shot posture on the ground, while the top inserts his dick from above—only not standing over his partner looking

Both going in opposite directions with the same goal in mind

into his face, but facing away from him instead. You could even say he was a truck towing his trailer bottom all the way to orgasm. This isn't the easiest of positions, though. Facing in opposite directions not only has the effect of forcing the top's wang into its socket at a very steep angle, it also means that the guy on the bottom can bend the penis coupling downwards by lowering his pelvis.

This begs the question: who is towing whom? All know is, I'd be happy to "hitch up" anytime.

▼ In–Out!

▷ Doggy Style

Mounting your lover from behind like a dog—that's doing it doggy style. The bottom crouches down on all fours and offers his ass up, while his lover kneels down behind him and gets down to business. You could fill entire volumes with this position alone. Eighty percent of the animal world mates this way, and there's a large gay majority that likes to pound it like a pooch. With good reason. Doggie style is the perfect position for quick, hard fucking, and the stability of this position provides you with plenty of opportunities to experiment. With quick grab at his partner's crotch, the top can dial the action with a bit of extra wanking. Or else he can prop himself up on his partner's ass and hump away from a squatting

position. The bottom can arch his back and push his ass back into his lover's crotch or lower his head, resting it on his forearms. It's not always a dog's life.

▶ Scissoring

If you're still doubtful that sex can be an art form, scissoring is the ultimate proof. Both partners' bodies interlock, their legs dovetailed like open scissors. Push as far as you can, until your balls collide, which feels great in itself. I, for one, could spend hours in this position, just rubbing my crotch into the other guy until I cum, but we've got other plans now. The scissoring position is actually a fucking position. All you need to do is push both your dicks into each other's butts. Then you start rocking back and forth. It's best if one of you

directs this, so that you don't disturb the rhythm. This one's really special. Exclusive in every way. But here's the catch: this ultimate form of erotic congress will only work if both of your dicks are only half erect when you insert them. You won't be able to bend a fully erect boner far enough, and guys with shorter cocks could have trouble, too. But that's no reason not to try out the scissor position. I've found that it's no less intense if only one guy gets penetrated, and that will definitely work out. Snippety snap!

▶ Suspended Congress

The *Kama Sutra* is chock full of ambitious poses. This is one of them. For the suspended congress, the top leans against the wall while his lover wraps his arms around his neck, draws his legs up, and hangs in front of the top's chest like a baby monkey. OK, not quite. He has his feet propped up against the wall and the top's rod in his anus, while the top supports his ass with his hands. Once you've achieved this, take a quick break for some passionate kissing and biting. Love bites play an important role in the *Kama Sutra.* As does scratching and biting. The marks all of this leaves behind are both a status symbol and a key erotic stimulus. But that's only by the way. Apart from that, suspended congress is a very intimate and tender position, but it does require a lot of stamina and strong biceps on the part of the top. Instead of thrusting hard with the hips, the basic motion consists of gently raising and lowering the bottom. By bending and stretching his legs, the monkey man can add to the action. While you're fucking, move away from the wall and shift the action to an armchair or the edge of your bed. This will turn the entire acrobatic affair into an adorable monkey embrace, whose innocent charms I have always appreciated very much. And so I leave you with this position and shall bring this chapter to a close.

Circle Jerk, Sandwich, Pyramid: Positions for Group Sex

Besides trying out new positions, there is another way you can introduce new impulses to gay congress: enter the third man. Or else the fourth or the fifth or .... Couples who have already tried a number of things out and are looking for new challenges may discover new aspects of their sexual needs by inviting other people to join in their sex lives. But these new constellations do require a certain amount of open-mindedness, curiosity, and self-confidence if you want to avoid jealousy. Mutual pleasure should be your goal, not sexual achievement. But do I need to tell you this? At this point, you are all experts in the *Gayma Sutra* method of relaxation. So let's take a look at some of the group sex positions.

▶ The Entrance Exam

A good way of extending your sex life to include a third man is to start out by leaving all the work to him. However, you should still make him feel welcome and included. In other words, place him literally in the center. The new guy should lie on his back with his hosts lying on either side of him, beating both of them off at the same time. This double wank allows the third man to demonstrate his manual dexterity, while giving him the chance to test his playmates' sex mentality: fast, hard, or gentle? You'll soon find out.

▶ The Circle Jerk

The advantages of a threesome are self-evident: you can fuck and blow at the same time. Or be fucked and blown. Or be fucked while having your taint licked. Depending on your position. But you should all agree on this beforehand. If two of you want the same thing, you'll just have to switch around. The greatest risk for a threesome is when only two of the participants get off while the other feels neglected. But in this case, it's up to him to point this

out. These ground rules should be negotiated before you get going, for example during a leisurely circle jerk. It sounds stupid, but that's the way it is. If you don't immediately jump all over each other, then that is both a sign of respect and a way to heighten your anticipation. Savor the thought of the next point on the agenda, for example the ...

▶ The Blow Job Triangle

What the 69 is to couples' foreplay, the Blow Job Triangle is to the threesome. The trio lies on the bed, head-to-dick and dick-to-head, indulging in three-way fellatio. Every hungry mouth is filled, there's naked skin everywhere you touch and everyone is in contact with everyone else. A fully comprehensive embrace, which of course works just as well with more people. The Blow Job Square, the Blow Job Pentagon, the Blow Job Hexagon ... the sky's the limit. Increas-

ing the number of players will, of course, heat up the general arousal, but the head-to-dick principle will ensure that the psychological community effect is maintained. When everyone is connected, nobody is excluded. All you can suck!

▶ **Three Cheers for the Blow Job Brigade**

Four hands can do more than two, and two mouths can swallow more than one. This formula sums up the blow job brigade, which is actually a combination of two positions. One person lies flat on his back, the second kneels over his face like a figurehead, feeding him his balls, while the third takes care of his dick from the front. In this constellation, the workload is very clearly distributed: the guy kneeling down takes care of the dick, the guy lying down pays attention to the balls, and the guy in the middle just needs to relax and enjoy. Just a tip for beginners: gently thrust towards the guy

blowing you while the other guy has his balls in his mouth and the tension in your sac will feel great.

▶ The Double Blow Job

Every gay man should try having two dicks in his mouth at least once in his life. Obviously, you're going to need three people. And here's the ideal starting position for this exercise: the scissors. We discussed this position in the last chapter, but here's a quick recap: the first guy's crotch straddles the second guy's crotch so that their balls touch. Then, the third man will take advantage of this entanglement by bringing his buddies' dicks together and beating them both off at the same time. And massaging them. And then finally getting busy with his lips around the big double package. And what if he can't fit the entire two-pack into his mouth? No prob-

lem. Then someone else can have a go. This is another advantage of group sex. If one of you isn't up to the task, you can always deputize someone else.

▷ Behind the Knees—Three-Star Version

You'll recall the fucking-the-backs-of-the-knees position in our foreplay chapter. There is, of course, a three-star, or rather, three guy version of this. This one is another classic example of a situation that can be made much hotter by adding a third man. One guy lies on his back in the middle with his legs bent, while his bedmates take up their positions on either side of him and slide their dicks into the gap behind his knees. That way, they'll not only be banging the guy in the middle, but also thrusting towards each other. The middleman can watch them both while he takes care of himself. Extra spice is added whenever both studs' bump dicks in the middle. Use plenty of lube for a smooth and enjoyable fuck.

▶ Chop and Change!

Many things are possible, but no man can fuck two other guys at the same time. Which means that in every threesome, there's always one guy who has to go unfucked. This is a great pity, but if you think about it, it applies to twosomes as well. So don't worry about it, just find a way to compensate. The best way consists of regularly switching around, but it's often enough to just include the third man by giving him some tender, loving care. Sometimes, anticipation can be even better than the real thing.

► The Sandwich

It's a legend, a myth, a mind-blowing experience. The famed sandwich features in the wet dreams of millions of gay men around the globe. That's a fact. But it's also a fact that when presented with the opportunity to enjoy a three-man fuck with a double-plus, most people are completely overwhelmed. And afterwards, many people are disappointed to realize that reality does not always live up to their expectations. All I can say is: never stop dreaming. Your first sandwich will always be prone to beginner's mistakes. It takes a bit of practice get the full benefits from this position. The much coveted position in the middle in particular can be a problem for many. Here are a couple of tips: Be sure to use plenty of lube on all the holes in

use! Penetration should proceed from front to back! Let the guy in the middle initiate the movement! When you start out, make sure only one of you initiates the thrusts—first because your movements will be carried over to the other two anyway, and second, because you need to find a common rhythm in several stages! Try out different variations—you can do the sandwich standing up or lying down, hands-free or tightly entwined, on your backs, your front, your sides ...! Play around and, above all, have fun!

▷ **Double Penetration**

Did I say every gay man should try having two dicks in his mouth at least once in his life? This raises the fully justified question: and then what? Logically, the next step after a double blow job and a sandwich would of course be: double penetration—that is, simultaneously plunging two shlongs into one anus. Not an absolute must, in my opinion, but I get why some people are fascinated. Depending on the size and length of the dicks in question, penetration can be quite easy or quite hard, but possible. There are of course a billion different ways of doing this, but I've narrowed them down to three that definitely work.

- **The scissors:** Just as you did for the double oral, have the two guys with a dick in the game scissor their legs so that their nuts touch and you can grab both their cocks together. One of them props himself up a little so that his erection is a little higher than the other guy's. The bottom squats down over the double dick and slides the higher one into his hole first. At the same time, he stretches his sphincter with his finger, for which he then substitutes dick number two.

- **One cowboy, two stallions:** By adding a third man, you can very easily turn the classic frontal cowboy position into a double-penetration-frontal-and-reverse-cowboy-position. The best place to do this is the edge of a bed or chair. Stallion number one spreads his legs so that stallion number two can stand between them and

join in the fun from below. The cowboy can assist him by leaning forward slightly.

- **The Backward Penetrator:** The bottom performs an anal backward roll and two guys capable of getting their erect dicks in a vertical position penetrate him from above. To be honest, this version is a complete mystery to me and I've only seen it done in porn. In the Hot House double feature *Black-N-Blue* the late Kent North did the backward roll and had Rafael Alencar and Marc Williams penetrate him.

Professional action performed by a fisting bottom and two semierect double-x dicks. You'll have to do a lot of casting to get this combination. And I hope this is absolutely clear now as I don't want to raise any false hopes: if you're not an anal veteran, you won't stand a chance with any of these three methods. The same goes for anyone who isn't pre-stretched. I don't want to rain on your parade, but I think it's a mistake to put pressure on yourself in extreme sports like this one. So if double penetration is an indispensable part of your gay raison d'être, do please give yourself plenty of time and take the lessons presented by the anal oracle in our sex gym chapter to heart.

▷ **The Stairs**

The Stairs are another aesthetic construction frequently used by the porn aesthete Kristen Bjorn in his films. This motif has as little in common with the chaotic splintering off that occurs during group sex parties in real life as if does with unbridled lust, but as it's a user-friendly concept, we'll go into it briefly. The underlying structure for this collective position is an actual staircase (a spiral staircase will do very nicely), with the steps stacked with lasciviously panting gentlemen, who use the difference in height to ensure they are at eye level with each other's genitalia. No climbing, just cumming. At eye level! And that's enough of that.

▶ The Daisy Chain

There's always an end to everything, except the sandwich! This kind of sums up the following mode of upscaling the three-layer-fuck principle to encompass an unlimited number of people and allow for a mass fulfillment of the predominant gay desire to be in the middle of it.

The group sex chain is a popular motif in porn and occasionally at puerile sex parties. Its satisfying aspects are due less to any really sensual qualities the experience might hold (which are not earth-shattering, in my opinion) and more to their psychological attraction: the knowledge that your dick is stuck in another guy's ass, while at the same time there's another dick in your own ass becomes, depending on the length of the group sex chain, exaggerated until you are convinced that all five, ten, or fifty guys behind you have their dicks stuck in your ass, while at the same time you're fuck-

Get in line! Don't be the weakest link in the chain!

ing all five, ten, or fifty guys in front of you. After all, everyone is connected in some way. It's a bit naive, but kind of touching all the same. So, get in line!

▷ The Pyramid

Let's raise the stakes even higher. The pyramid is a somewhat old-fashioned group sex tableau whose attractions lie mainly in its impressive architecture and its for the most part hierarchical structure. The orgy organizer or master of ceremonies should stand on a table or a plinth, like a naked Renaissance king. One man kneels in front of him, sucking his dick, while another guy behind him licks his ass, and two more guests on either side nibble and suck at his nipples. This should make it clear beyond any doubt who is at the top of the sexual food chain and how the same principle is followed at the lower levels. Because the asses and dicks of these men, whom I shall call "subjects," are attended to by eager servants of lust, and the sweaty, sticky priapic pyramid gets broader and broader toward the base—depending on the number of guests. At best, orgasms should also take place in hierarchical order—cascading from the top to the bottom. Of course, it's highly unlikely that this would ever work in reality, but a guy can dream, can't he?

The more the merrier—the pyramid should be performed on a grand scale.

Rim-Seat Chin-up & Sling-Swing: The Sexy Seven Positions Involving Gadgets

Whether you swear by sex gimmicks, accessories, and toys or avoid them like the plague—no one will deny that they can help you broaden your sexual horizons. But that's not all. Some positions aren't even feasible without using some kind of gadget or other aid. I'm not talking about the tables, chairs, and beds we've used to accomplish some of the positions described here and where I'm just going to assume that most of you have them standing around somewhere or other. No, I'm talking about sex toys that are absolutely essential for certain positions to work. There's more than you'd think. Here's an overview of the "Sexy Seven."

▼ Double Dildo: The Plough

In the not terribly uncommon case that your supposedly versatile date turns out to be a grade A passive bottom, it's a good idea to keep a double dildo around—at least, if you happen to be a bottom yourself. The point of the whole thing should be obvious: a silicon penis with a tip at both ends will enable you to satisfy not only your guest's anal appetite, but your own as well. At the same time! It sounds easier than it actually is, but whether you do it standing up, squatting, or doggy style, it can be a real eye-opener. The plough is a variation on doggy style. Bottom number one gets down on all fours and his partner sticks one tip of the dildo in his butt and then bottom number two does the same to himself with the other end. Whether you do this squatting or kneeling down depends on how experienced bottom number two is. In any case, both participants should end up kneeling on the ground, ass to ass, connected by the dildo. The picture on the Levi's label might serve as a visual reference: the one with the two horses pulling a pair of jeans in different directions in order to show how durable they are. The difference being that for the plow, the two horses aren't driven apart, but rather towards each other. The moment when both asses meet, and the double dildo disappears up to the hilt on both sides is sheer magic. But it can't be done with the very long dildos, which are the exception in the category of double dildos, anyway.

More of a cautious sliding back and forth than a wild smacking of ass on ass, but the gentle rhythm makes it a very intimate experience.

▼ Belt: Fucking with Reins

Here's a "sex toy" nearly all of you will have at home, without being aware of its potential: a plain belt. Preferably made out of leather, there are countless ways you can use this to pimp out an average fuck to style and finesse. Fucking with reins is best done doggie style. If the top wraps the belt around the hips or thighs of the guy in front of him (or even clenched between his teeth) and steers by tightening or slackening the reins, you can turn this into a really hot and rhythmic choreography whose boundaries can be pushed to infinity if your top has the energy. A brief warning: another popular use of the belt noose is as a collar. Rightly enough, but please try this out only with someone who is both prudent and trustworthy, someone who won't pull too tightly in the heat of the moment and cut off your breathing. If this is the point of the entire exercise, I still stand by my warning.

▼ Rim Seat: The Rim-Seat-Chin-Up

Rim seats are detached toilet seats that you sit on so that your partner can lick your ass from underneath. You can purchase these things for a ridiculous amount of money from any well-stocked BDSM store, or you can just make your own by sawing a circular hole out of the seat of a kitchen chair, or simply removing the upholstery. If you're a perfectionist, you can also attach a toilet seat to the frame, but you won't necessarily need to for the rim-seat-chin-up. The rimmer holds on the chair with both hands and uses his arms to pull himself up to his partner's hole. The latter should spread his ass cheeks, he won't get much out of it otherwise. If your arms get tired (and they will tire quickly at this angle), you can use a cushion to support your head and neck. Rimming can be a pleasurable and comfortable activity for both participants.

▼ Sling: The Sling-Swing

The sling's reputation as a utensil reserved for fetishists is presumably attributable to the fact that fetishists tend to invest more time and money into their sex lives, and that they therefore have a more pronounced need and willingness to invest a fair amount of cash in a "love swing" than most other people. But basically everyone should try having sex in and with a sling at least once. First of all, it's incredibly comfortable, and second, it's a mind-blowing experience for everyone concerned. With the bottom lying in the sling with his legs strapped up and the top gently pushing him back and forth with a few well-placed thrusts of his hips, you'll soon reach an exquisite feeling of sexual weightlessness. Which is why for a long time I thought it would be romantic if the top held onto the chains while swinging back and forth and took his feet off the ground for a mid-air fuck. But once I'd tried it out, it didn't seem quite as romantic. For one thing, holding on is a real pain in the ass, for another, once you've "taken off," there's not much more in the way of thrusting. So I suggest you simply find ways to vary the standard move, with the top standing in front of the sling and using its swinging motion to complement his own thrusts. By the way: detachable sex slings with fabric straps may be a lot cheaper and even a bit more flexible than their big leather brothers, but you won't have had the full sling-swing experience until you've tried the leather.

▼ Butt Machine: License to Fuck

Charles Bukowski coined the term and the online portal "Butt Machine Boys" turned it into a wet dream for gay bottoms: the fucking machine. For a couple hundred bucks, you can now buy one of these gadgets from fetish suppliers such as the established US-based store Mr. S and you can use it in every conceivable position and thrust frequency. I have to admit that purchasing one of these machines for myself has always been too expensive for me, but I've been told that playing with all the speeds is akin to getting your license to fuck, and the best way to celebrate is doing it doggy style. I'll be sure to remember this when the time comes; in the meantime, I'll just wait it out in the missionary position.

▼ Fleshjack: Motion on a Mission

What started out as the bright idea of producing a masturbatory device shaped like a flashlight has grown into veritable wanker's paradise, where different positions also play an increasingly important role. Some fleshjacks can be stuck to the shower wall with suction cups for hands-free penetration (Fleshlight shower mount), and you can also get stools especially designed for the purpose with holes you can stick your Fleshjack in if you want to do it doggy style (Motion Top Dog). My personal favorite is the Motion on a Mission footstool, which reduces the benefits of the missionary position to its mechanical qualities and whose ergonomic designed ramped shape invites you to lean in and start thrusting.

▼ The Excercise Bike: Riding the IT

The IT was inspired by the *South Park* episode "The Entity," where Mr. Garrison invents the monowheel IT, which is driven by an anal-oral system, with one dildo-shaped handle stuck in the user's mouth and another in his ass. Completely silly of course, but it still got me wondering where you could actually have sex on an exercise bike. I probably came up with the idea because my previously mentioned ex had bought one of these things and I thought I'd give it a more profound function than the one it already had. Personally, I think cycling on a exercise bike is a pointless relocation of the original activity to an indoor space, but now that I've taken a ride on the IT, I have the greatest respect for this home exercise gadget. The basic principle is this: the top sits on the saddle with his lover sitting over him with the top's dick plugged into his ass and his feet on the bike's base. The bottom then holds onto the handlebars while his partner starts pedaling with his legs slightly spread.

The result is a subtle back-and-forth motion of his dick in his buddy's hole, caused by the pedal-pusher's thighs going up and down and hindered only by the fact that both of them have to constantly work on keeping their balance. Purchasing an exercise bike solely for the purpose of an IT ride would therefore be taking it a bit too far—but if you've already got one, you might want to try it out.

One More Round?—Afterword

Was that it, already? Well, I just asked myself the same question. A moment ago we were in the middle of Suspended Congress and the next moment it's all over and we're back to everyday life. Books are no different from sexual encounters. First they pump you up full of expectations and then it's over far too quickly. I fully realize that one or another of you will be complaining because I didn't include as many positions as you'd expected. Or because the first positions you tried out didn't work. Or because I left out your favorite position. Or else ... it's all possible. Although, I would check the part about your favorite position. In this area of endeavor, names can be a bit tricky. Only the really big classics like the 69, the missionary, or doggy style have really well-established names and these are usually universally understood. But what about the others? One source calls it the "Crooked Piston," another the "Lateral Coxcomb" and yet another the "Discarded Pickle." I ended up calling it Tom Wolfe's "Leg-Lock." While checking out all the names, I got confused after a while, so in the end I simply took the liberty of making up my own names for a number of positions. I'm OK with that, after all, the *Gayma Sutra* isn't the *Kama Sutra* and gay sex culture has its own rituals, mannerisms, and codes. So why shouldn't we have our own names? And concerning the number of positions: if you count the top ten packages as single positions, which in the final analysis they are, you'll end up with the very pleasing number of ninety-nine sex positions. And if you included the wheelbarrow described in the preface, then that's one hundred. That should be enough. Nor do I think I've left out anything of the utmost importance.

And that's enough self-criticism. Because I actually feel pretty good about where I am and how I got here. For me, finishing up a book project is like saying good-bye after a first date. If it went well, you always think of a million other things you could have said or done or even tried out. Applying this feeling to the *Gayma Sutra*, I can definitely say that there's a lot more things I could have said. Who knows? Perhaps I'll write the *Gayma Sutra* parts two to ten and in the end I'll have written the complete gay version of the great book of love, the one I always wanted as a teenager. In due time ... For now, I'm eager to see what the finished book will look like. And I'm definitely looking forward to performing the *Gayma Sutra* initiation rite with it. By the way, this is a good time to close the circle and take a look at the status quo. We've done the theoretical part. Now it's time for the page-ripping practical bit. Stick to those passages in this book that caught your interest, slip a marker in at those places and read them just before your next date. Or perhaps you just want to prove that your humble author was just too clumsy to do the helicopter with grace and precision and that you could do a much better job. That's absolutely fine by me. As long as there's something going on in the gay bedroom and it's more than routine fucking and keeping up a cool facade, I'm OK with it. This book has nothing to do with the rest of it. If all you want to do is look cool, you won't be able to try out any of the positions. In fact, you won't be able to try out anything at all. But trying things out is what makes life interesting, isn't it? So, if you want me, I'll be on the next page in our Game-A-Sutra play area.

Apart from that, enjoy yourself and rip a few pages!
Axel Neustädter

Ideal Combination! Elephant Craig Reynolds and Stallion John Magnum in Score—Game2

Bonus Material: Game-A-Sutra

I made you a promise and I'll keep it. Here it is: the card game based on the compatibility test on page 25. You could play it during the breaks between positions or even as a playful warm-up before getting started. After all, it is about dick and hole sizes and what they can teach us. Here are the rules of the game!

▷ Preparation

- Cut out the twenty-four cards with the animal, ass and penis symbols on them and spread them out face down on an even surface.
- Cut out the eleven cards with the arrow symbols. Pile them in a stack, which you then place to one side.
- Open this book to the sexual compatibility chart on page 25 and place this to one side as well.

▷ Objective

The "Game-A-Sutra" is designed to teach you more about the high, low and ideal sexual matches of the *Kama Sutra*. The objective is to collect as many pairs of cards as possible and at the same time to memorize the dick and hole sizes and their corresponding animal symbols. This is just a lighthearted game, but it also aims at making the at-the-first-glance-rather-confusing compatibility model a bit more understandable. I've already explained my personal stance towards how the respective matches are classified in the "Pole Position" chapter. So I don't want any dick or ass complexes here. You shouldn't play games with those.

▷ Playing the Game

- Each player takes a card from the stack of arrow cards and places it face up in front of him. The direction the arrow points in shows which type of match you're looking for. For example, an arrow pointing upwards requires the "highest" match (i.e. stallion/size L dick and doe/size S hole), and a horizontal arrow indicates an "ideal match" of which there are three different versions. Use the chart on page 21 as a memory aid.

- The youngest player begins. One move consists of turning up two cards on the table. If the face up dick-animal/hole-animal combinations correspond to the arrow card, the play can take those cards out of the game and keep them. It doesn't matter if you combine a body motif with an animal motif, body motif with a body motif, or an animal motif with an animal motif. As long as they correspond to the arrow card. Place the cards you have won to the side, next to the used arrow card. Then take a new arrow card and it's your turn again. If you turn up a card combination that doesn't correspond to the new arrow card, the other players get a second to memorize the motifs and then the cards are placed face down again. And then it's the next player's turn.

- The game is over once the last arrow card has been used. At this point, there will be one more pair of motif cards left, which the players can light-heartedly interpret as a reflection on their own sexual compatibility if they like. The player with the most cards has won.

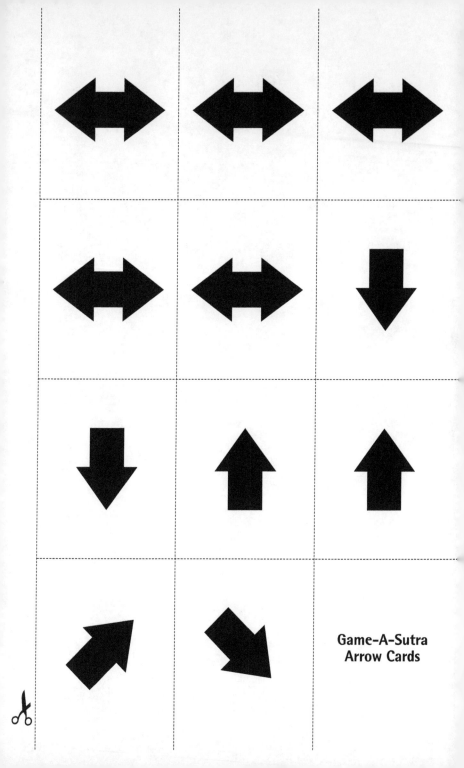

Game-A-Sutra
Arrow Cards

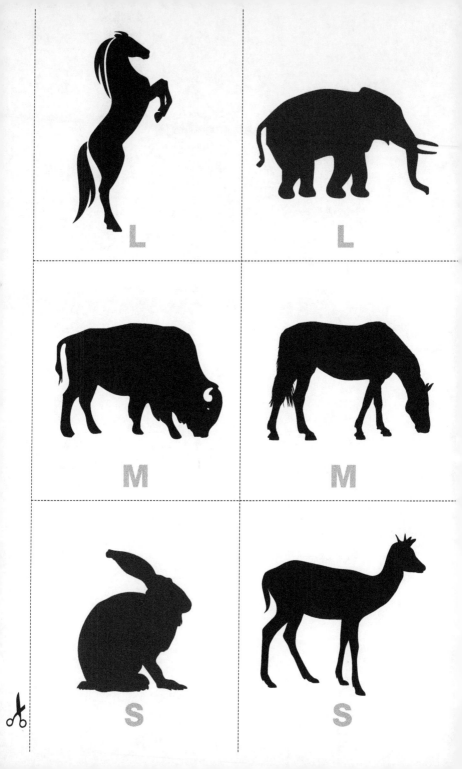

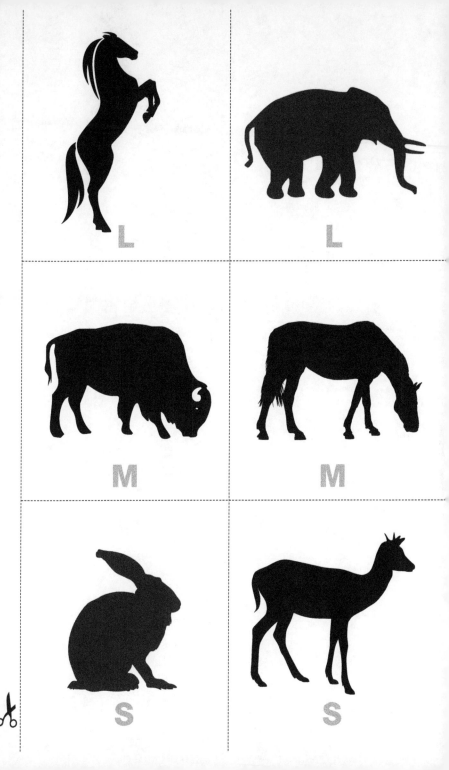

L

L

M

M

S

S

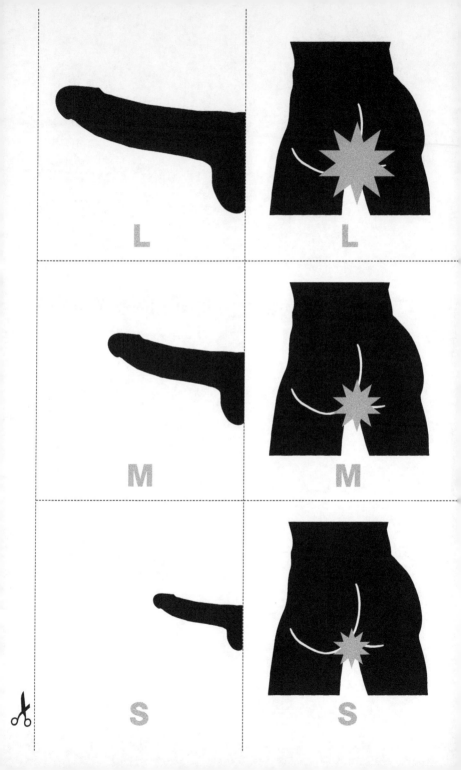

L   L

M   M

S   S

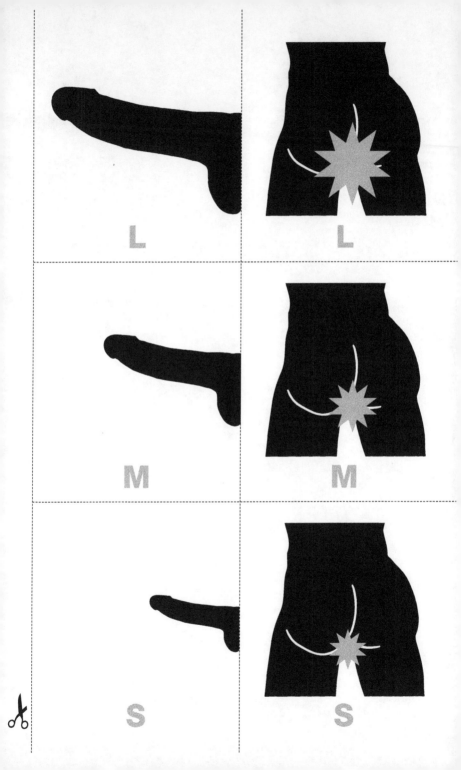

L   L

M   M

S   S

Photo Credits

RonAmato.com
65

BelAmiOnline.com
Cover and back cover Foto, 7,
15, 25, 37, 43, 43, 75, 92, 94-
103, 108, 113, 114, 119, 122,
128, 131, 137, 138, 134, 145,
147, 150, 152-156, 159, 165

Fank Bell /
Thevirtuosopianist.org
84

BigDipperJelly.com
29

ButchDixon.com
30

CockyBoys.com
32, 55, 109, 158,

CorbinFisher.com
67

ColtStudioGroup.com
34

DaveyWavey.tv
35

FalconStudios.com
26, 28, 44, 59, 62

Fleshjack.com
170

HotHouse.com
16, 31, 33, 38, 47, 49, 57, 71,
73, 77, 86, 88, 89, 107, 118,
125, 127, 135, 139, 149, 157,
161, 163, 174

iStock.com
Grafik:
Hase, Hengst und Reh: 19, 21,
179, 181
Stimmungssymbole Hantel,
Herz, Würfel, Uhr, Flasche 24
u.a.
Fotos: 51, 171

Jalifstudio.com
169

MisterB.com
69, 166, 168

RagingStallion.com
127, 133

1stClassMale.co.uk
81

Everything a Man Needs to Know

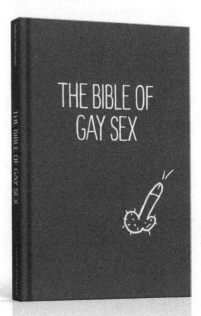

Stephan Niederwieser
THE BIBLE OF GAY SEX
272 pages, softcover,
6¾ x 9½"
17 x 24 cm,
978-3-86787-447-2
US$ 32.99 / £ 19.99

Hallelujah! Finally there is a book that tells you ALL you need
to know about gay sex. For let's be honest: Talking sex is only
easy as long as you can play the part of the experienced lover.
Stephan Niederwieser—author of various sex guides—informs
you about everything you need to know, whether it's dating,
health, the best ways to relax or the responsible use of stimu-
lants. *The Bible of Gay Sex* is richly illustrated; it's a competent
and entertaining book about everyone's favorite pastime.

A Sexy Guide for Sexy Encounters

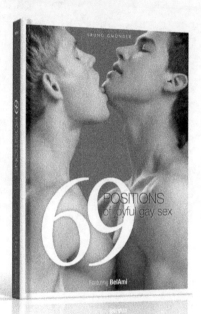

Bel Ami
69 POSITIONS OF
JOYFUL GAY SEX
6¾ x 9½"
17,5 x 24,5 cm,
978-3-86787-261-4
US$ 61.99 / £ 34.99

Beyond doggy style and the missionary position there are
countless possibilities to enjoy sex between men. In this book
the popular Bel Ami models Kris Evans and Dolph Lambert
present 69 of them—each and every single one an opportunity
to provide some fresh inspiration to your love life.

Handsome Bel Ami models present the various positions; brief
texts give competent information on how to perform each position and everything else you should consider.
69 Positions of Joyful Gay Sex is illustrating, erotic and
enlightening.

Model: Jake Bass

COCKYBOYS.COM

Angel Rock

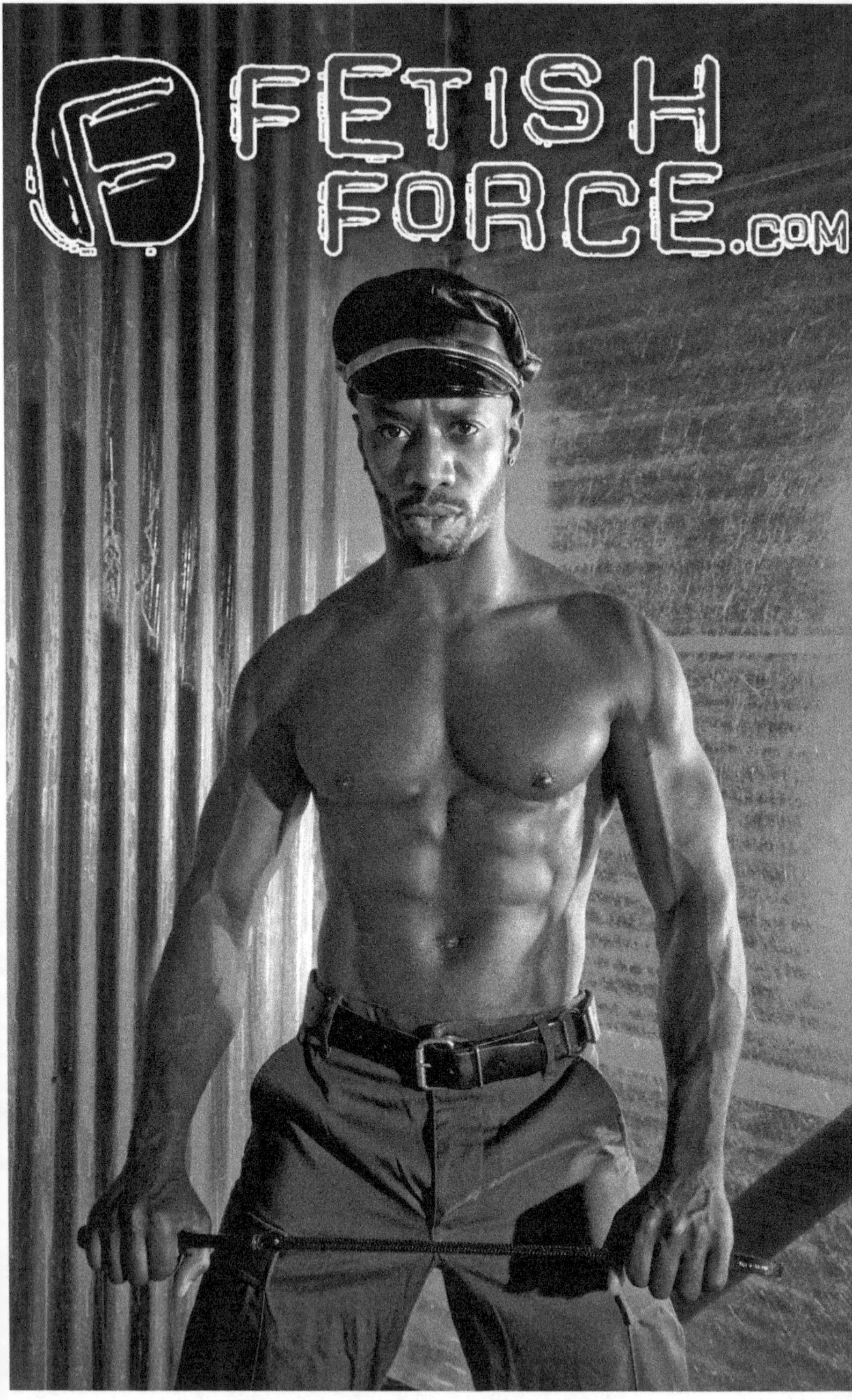
FETISH
FORCE.COM